QuickCook

QuickCook
Midweek Meals

Recipes by Emma Jane Frost and Nichola Palmer

Every dish, three ways—you choose!
30 minutes | 20 minutes | 10 minutes

An Hachette UK Company
www.hachette.co.uk

First published in Great Britain in 2013 by Hamlyn,
a division of Octopus Publishing Group Ltd
Endeavour House, 189 Shaftesbury Avenue, London WC2H 8JY
www.octopusbooksusa.com

Copyright © Octopus Publishing Group Ltd 2013

Distributed in the US by Hachette Book Group USA
237 Park Avenue, New York NY 10017 USA

Distributed in Canada by Canadian Manda Group
165 Dufferin Street, Toronto, Ontario, Canada M6K 3H6

ISBN 978-0-600-62774-6

Printed and bound in China

10 9 8 7 6 5 4 3 2 1

Standard level kitchen spoon and cup measurements are used in all recipes.

Ovens should be preheated to the specified temperature. If using a convection oven,
follow the manufacturer's instructions for adjusting the time and temperature.
Broilers should also be preheated.

This book includes dishes made with nuts and nut derivatives. It is advisable for
those with known allergic reactions to nuts and nut derivatives and those who may
be potentially vulnerable to these allergies, such as pregnant and nursing mothers,
people with weakened immune systems, the elderly, babies, and children, to avoid
dishes made with nuts and nut oils.

It is also prudent to check the labels of prepared ingredients for the possible inclusion
of nut derivatives.

The U.S. Department of Agriculture (USDA) advises that eggs should not be consumed
raw. This book contains some dishes made with raw or lightly cooked eggs. It is
prudent for more vulnerable people, such as pregnant and nursing mothers, people
with weakened immune systems, the elderly, babies, and young children, to avoid
uncooked or lightly cooked dishes made with eggs.

Contents

Introduction

30 20 10—Quick, Quicker, Quickest

This book offers a new and flexible approach to planning meals for busy cooks and lets you choose the recipe option that best fits the time you have available. Inside you will find 360 dishes that will inspire you and motivate you to get cooking every day of the year. All the recipes take a maximum of 30 minutes to cook. Some take as little as 20 minutes and, amazingly, many take only 10 minutes. With a little preparation, you can easily try out one new recipe from this book each night and slowly you will build a wide and exciting portfolio of recipes to suit your needs.

How Does it Work?

Every recipe in the QuickCook series can be cooked one of three ways—a 30-minute version, a 20-minute version, or a superquick-and-easy 10-minute version. At the beginning of each chapter you'll find recipes listed by time. Choose a dish based on how much time you have and turn to that page.

You'll find the main recipe at the top of the page with a beautiful photograph and two variations by time below.

If you enjoy the dish, you can go back and cook the other time options. If you liked the 30-minute Apple and Peach Marzipan Slice (see pages 270–271), but only have 10 minutes to spare, then you'll find a way to cook it using quick ingredients or clever shortcuts. Alternatively, browse through all the 360 recipes, find something that takes your eye, and then cook the version that fits your time frame.

If you love the ingredients and flavors of the 10-minute Tomato and Mozzarella Sourdough Bruschetta (see pages 200–201), why not try the 20-minute Warm Tomato and Mozzarella Salad with Sourdough Croutons, or be inspired to cook a more elaborate dish using similar ingredients, such as the 30-minute Baked Tomato and Mozzarella Sourdough.

Or, for easy inspiration, turn to the gallery on pages 12–19 to get an instant overview by themes, such as Mediterranean Flavors and Spicy Favorites.

QuickCook Online

To make life even easier, you can use the special code on each recipe page to e-mail yourself a recipe card for printing, or e-mail a text-only shopping list to your phone. Go to www.hamlynquickcook.com and enter the recipe code at the bottom of each page.

 MID-DESS-MOB

Midweek Meals

Life is busy. Most of us have to work, be it inside or outside the home, part time or full time, and walking into a kitchen on a weekday evening with half-empty cupboards and no idea of what you are going to cook for dinner is a dispiriting and stressful way to end the day. Having to defrost chicken breasts or run out for some bouillon cubes in order to begin a recipe can take the enjoyment out of what may otherwise have been quite a therapeutic, enjoyable activity.

For many, cooking in the week is boring; it is a "must-do" activity instead of a "like-to-do" activity. Energy and creativity levels are low, there's little time, and there are other things you need to be getting on with. So we have come up with this book to put the pleasure back into cooking meals midweek. We believe that no matter how little time you have, cooking should be a creative, therapeutic, and enjoyable process with an end result you can be proud of. However, we are realistic; we know time is tight—there is paperwork to do after dinner and the house needs cleaning before your guests arrive tomorrow. So we've come up with a whole array of inspiring meals—360 in total—to tantalize your taste buds and kick-start your creativity, and, what's more, every single one of them can be prepared and cooked in half an hour or less!

Like the other books in Hamlyn's QuickCook series, this book provides you with 120 recipes, each of which can be prepared in 30, 20, or even just 10 minutes. And because the time that you have available to cook varies each day, and because we cooks can get bored easily with a limited recipe repertoire, we have included two variations for each recipe, both of which are superfast and taste fantastic.

Plan Healthy Balanced Meals

Some "food-in-a-hurry"-style cookbooks assume you have an army of helpers in your kitchen and an array of special gadgets and equipment to speed up the prep process. We make no such assumptions. We do suggest, however, that you will take a little time to plan and buy for your dishes, because the key to midweek meal success is preparation. Use some of your lunch hour or some time at the weekend to browse through this book and choose four or five meals that you'd like to serve in the week. Then, once you've worked out what ingredients you need, make sure you get everything in stock ready for the beginning of the week. Don't forget Internet shopping and home-delivery services—they are designed for busy people and can be arranged for times that suit you and your busy schedule.

Mix It Up

It may seem obvious, but when you are planning your week's meals, try to get a good balance of different foods on your plate each day and through the week. We have planned the recipes in this book to help give you a broad range of nutrient-dense foods across the week, but the key is to mix up your menus and not always cook the same types of food. We would suggest that you keep the following in mind when you are creating your meal plan:

- Eat fish at least twice a week because it is known to reduce heart disease, is rich in the B and D vitamins, and contains high levels of Omega 3, which is great for your heart.
- Chicken can be eaten as often as your budget allows, but try to buy organic where possible.
- If you are a red meat addict, choose lean cuts where possible and cuts that lend themselves to quick cooking. Limit red meat to twice a week.
- Organ meats are an excellent source of vitamins, copper, iron, and zinc; however, the liver accumulates chemical residues from the animal, so limit your intake to once a week.
- Nuts and seeds are nutritional gems. They are low in saturated fats, high in protein and fiber, and are brimming with the B vitamins and many useful minerals.
- Eggs are a quick and healthy protein source and low in saturated fat—current thinking is that up to six eggs a week is a perfectly healthy addition to your diet.
- Mix up your vegetables as much as your budget allows. Include root and leafy vegetables and as many different colors as you can. All vegetables contain high levels of vitamin C, many contain important B vitamins, and all are

abundant in fiber. What's more, when they are cooked lightly and quickly, as many are in this book, their goodness is retained and their benefits are felt all the more.
- Always choose whole grains because these are good for your heart and keep you fuller for longer.

The Pantry

It helps if you keep your kitchen well stocked at all times so you only have to buy the fresh and just a few ingredients each week. For those who keep their cupboards lean, this can be a time-consuming and possibly expensive exercise initially, but it is worth it to keep costs down thereafter and to reduce time spent shopping each week.

To put together a magical meal in minutes, you need some basics in your cupboards. All-purpose flour and cornstarch, a container of instant milk for emergencies, cans of diced tomatoes, chickpeas and beans, tomato puree or sauce, tomato paste, strong English mustard, and a good selection of oils, including a basic vegetable oil, such as sunflower oil, a good-quality olive oil, and some more alternative flavors, such as peanut, sesame ,and walnut. Always have a good-quality balsamic vinegar in the cupboard, and, for those dishes with an Asian twist, stock up on coconut milk, soy sauce, Thai fish sauce, sweet chili dipping sauce and hoisin sauce, plus a selection of your preferred noodles and rice.

Don't be afraid to buy some "quick" ingredients for those superquick meals you're going to prepare: pesto sauces, store-bought pizza crusts, and Thai curry paste are must-haves for busy days, and don't forget you can buy garlic, ginger, and lemon grass in paste form, which can be quickly and easily squeezed into the pan when cooking.

Jars of preserved vegetables are a tasty, easy addition to many pastas, salads, and rice dishes, and can be stored for months (if not years) successfully as long as they are kept cool. Therefore, it would not go amiss to treat yourself to some jars of artichokes, olives, and roasted red peppers, and, to add the occasional kick to your cooking, keep some capers and anchovies in stock, too; you'd be surprised how much these tiny additions give to a meal.

You may not think of yourself as a gardener, but learning to keep a few herbs growing in flowerpots on the windowsill will be a greata boon when it comes to adding quick and easy flavor to a midweek meal. Easy-to-keep herbs include basil, cilantro, chives, and rosemary. Oregano and thyme can be a little trickier to grow; however, these can be bought fresh in bunches and frozen for when you need them. Don't be concerned if the leaves turn dark or black—they will retain their flavor.

The Refrigerator and Freezer

Make space in your refrigerator for some key ingredients that form the basis for many meals: onions, garlic, hard cheese, such as cheddar and a good strong Parmesan, a carton of crème fraîche or sour cream, and some plain or Greek yogurt. Keep quartered lemons and limes, ginger, and chiles in the freezer, plus nutrient-rich vegetables that freeze well, such as spinach, peas, or corn kernels. Bacon, chicken breasts, fish fillets, and sausages can be separated and frozen in small servings ready for easy defrosting; or buy bags of frozen shrimp, mussels, or mixed seafood for an easy addition to soups, stews, and stir-fries.

Remember, too, that bread freezes well; bags of muffins and burger buns kept in the freezer are sure to get good use; try the delicious cod burgers on page 170 or the irresistible Eggs Benedict on page 32 for some nutritious, fast, comfort food for all the family. When a loaf of bread is no longer fresh enough to eat in slices, blend up the loaf in a food processor and freeze the bread crumbs in small food bags ready for coating chicken or fish fillets. For an alternative way of using your bread crumbs, try our Backed Cheesy Zucchini on page 188—a surefire winner with the vegetarians in your family.

One Dish

Everyone will love these tasty one-dish wonders.

Easy Cassoulet 24

Creamy Pork, Apple, and Mustard Pan-Fry 54

Chorizo and Ham Eggs 70

Chicken and Corn Chowder 86

Thyme-Roasted Chicken and Carrots 102

Creamy Chicken, Ham, and Leek Pan-Fry 122

Crispy Pesto Baked Cod 130

Pan-Fried Herbed Salmon with Creamy Mascarpone Sauce 156

Pea, Leek, and Potato Soup with Pesto and Cheesy Toasts 182

Pan-Fried Caramel Apples 242

Spiced Pan-Fried Pineapple with Rum 252

Pan-Fried Marsala Fruit and Almonds 276

Last-Minute Entertaining

Inspiring and indulgent meals for special occasions.

Balsamic Lamb with Mashed
Parsnips and Potatoes 26

Steaks with Easy Braised
Red Cabbage and Blackberries 68

Chicken and Dolcelatte Pasta
Casserole 78

Mussels with Cider and Garlic
Sauce 128

Seafood Tagliatelle 146

Asparagus, Lemon, and
Herb-Stuffed Salmon 148

Scallop, Bacon, and Pine Nut
Pan-Fry 168

Asparagus, Eggplant, Brie, and
Tomato Quiche 204

Goat Cheese and Butternut
Squash Stuffed Peppers 212

Berry and White Chocolate
Tarts 246

Tropical Fruit and Coconut
Cheesecakes 258

Baked Chocolate Orange
Mousse 278

Mediterranean Flavors

Great meals that are packed with the fresh flavors of the Mediterranean.

2 Lamb Meatballs with Herbed Feta Couscous 30

3 Pepperoni, Artichoke, and Olive Pizzas 34

3 Prosciutto and Asparagus Tart 42

3 Risotto-Topped Lamb and Vegetable Casserole 66

3 Chicken Parmigiana 80

3 Greek Chicken Stifado 100

3 Spicy Squid with Fries and Garlic Mayo 134

3 Spinach and Feta Phyllo Packages 180

2 Mediterranean Tomato Soup 198

1 Tomato and Mozzarella Sourdough Bruschetta 200

1 Speedy Iced Tiramisu 234

2 Grilled Fruit Packages with Pistachio Yogurt 254

Spicy Favorites

Turn up the heat with this selection of hot and spicy recipes.

Moroccan Lamb Kebabs with Warm Chickpea Salad 50

Spiced Beef and Onion Chapattis 52

Paprika Chicken Quesadillas 88

Caribbean Chicken with Rice and Peas 92

Asian Chicken Satay Stir-Fry 114

Spicy Chicken and Plantain with Caribbean Sauce 116

Chicken Jalfrezi 118

Thai Crab Cakes with Carrot Noodle Salad 144

Shrimp Jambalaya 150

Chile Seafood Stew 162

Curried Cauliflower, Lentils, and Rice 184

Spiced Butternut Squash Soup 194

Low-Fat Meals

Healthy recipes that don't compromise on taste.

Thai Chicken and Vegetable Kebab Wraps 84

Mexican Chicken Burgers with Tomato Salad 94

Lemon and Parsley Chicken Skewers 96

Tuna and Bean Pasta Salad 132

Ginger and Lime Mackerel with Roasted Vegetables 136

Teriyaki Salmon with Egg Noodles 142

Thai Green Fish Curry with Lime Leaves 160

Asian Shrimp and Crab Stir-Fry 172

Roasted Carrot and Beet Pearl Barley with Feta 222

Baked Honeyed Figs and Raspberries 232

Roasted Plum and Orange Compote with Granola 236

Soft Raspberry Meringues 260

Midweek Energy Boosters

Give your energy levels a boost with these nutrient-packed dishes.

Warm Prosciutto, Chicken
Liver, and Walnut Salad 58

Pan-Fried Liver with Caper Sauce
and Mashed Vegetables 60

Sticky Soy Chicken with
Fruity Asian Salad 90

Warm Mediterranean Chicken
and Bulgur Wheat Salad 108

Chicken, Potato, and Spinach
Pan-Fry 110

Smoked Fish and Fennel
Casserole 152

Chile and Lemon
Fish Cakes 164

Falafels with Beet Salad and
Mint Yogurt 186

Baked Cheesy Zucchini 188

Stuffed Pasta, Pine Nut, and
Butternut Gratin 192

Chickpea, Artichoke, and
Tomato Pan-Fry 202

Pea, Parmesan, and Mint
Risotto 210

Feed the Family

Great-tasting recipes that everyone will enjoy.

2 Spicy Sausage and Arugula Pasta 28

2 Garlicky Pork with Warm Lima Bean Salad 36

3 Lamb and Chorizo Burgers with Roasted New Potatoes 40

3 Spicy Sausage, Rosemary, and Bean Stew 62

3 Beef, Squash, and Prune Stew 64

2 Creamy Chicken and Tarragon Pasta 98

3 Honeyed Chicken and Roasted Vegetables with Rosemary 120

3 Herbed Cod and Mashed Potatoes with Gruyère and Spinach 158

2 Red Lentils with Naan 216

2 Blueberry and Banana French Toast 250

3 Chocolate Cookie and Fruit Squares 256

2 Pan-Fried Peach and Plum Cinnamon Crunch 268

Just for Two

Special meals for just the two of you.

Eggs Benedict 32

Creamy Peppered Steaks with Sweet Potato Fries 38

Sausages in Red Wine with Creamy Layered Potatoes 56

Chicken, Pancetta, and Mushroom Carbonara 106

Roasted Chicken and Spiced Butternut Squash 112

Roasted Garlicky Herb Sea Bass, Fennel, and Potatoes 166

Juicy Cod Burgers with Tartar Sauce 170

Pan-Fried Proscuitto-Wrapped Salmon 174

Garlic and Herb Mushroom Tart 196

Molten Chocolate Lava Cakes 244

Apple and Peach Marzipan Slice 270

Pan-Fried Banana and Maple Syrup Brioche Rolls 274

QuickCook
Meat

Recipes listed by cooking time

3⦵

2⦵

10

30 Easy Cassoulet

Serves 4

2 tablespoons olive oil
4 Italian-style sausages
4 boneless, skinless chicken
  thighs, opened out flat
1 large onion, chopped
2 celery sticks, chopped
2 teaspoons smoked paprika
2 (14½ oz) cans diced tomatoes
  with garlic and herbs
2 (15 oz) cans cannellini beans,
  rinsed and drained
½ cup fresh white bread crumbs
2 tablespoons chopped parsley
salt and black pepper

- Heat 2 tablespoons of the oil in a large saucepan, add the sausages and chicken thighs, and sauté for 5 minutes, turning occasionally, until browned. Remove the meat from the pan and slice the sausages.

- Add the onion and celery to the saucepan and sauté for 2–3 minutes, until slightly softened. Add the paprika, stir well, and return the sausages and chicken to the pan. Add the tomatoes and beans and season. Bring to a boil, then reduce the heat, cover, and simmer for 20 minutes.

- Meanwhile, heat the remaining oil in a skillet, add the bread crumbs, and sauté, stirring, until golden. Serve the cassoulet sprinkled with the bread crumbs and parsley.

10 Smoky Sausage and Beans on Toast

Heat 2 tablespoons olive oil in a large saucepan, add 2 chopped onions, and sauté for 5 minutes, until softened. Add 2 (15 oz) cans baked beans, 2 tablespoons barbecue sauce, and 2 teaspoons Dijon mustard, then stir in 8 oz sliced smoked pork link sausages and heat through. Serve on thick slices of buttered wheat toast.

20 Chunky Sausage and Bean Soup

Heat 2 tablespoons olive oil in a large saucepan, add 2 chopped onions and 2 chopped celery sticks, and sauté for 5 minutes, until softened. Add 2 teaspoons smoked paprika, 2 (14½ oz) cans diced tomatoes, and 2 (15 oz) cans baked beans and bring to a boil, then reduce the heat and simmer for 10 minutes. Slice 8 oz smoked pork link sausages and stir into the soup. Heat through for 2 minutes, then serve with garlic bread.

Balsamic Lamb with Mashed Parsnips and Potatoes

Serves 2

1 parsnip, peeled and cut into chunks

3 Yukon gold or russet potatoes, peeled and cut into chunks

1 tablespoon olive oil

1 onion, cut into 6 wedges

2 lamb cutlets, about 5 oz each

½ cup red wine

1 teaspoon Dijon mustard

2 tablespoons balsamic vinegar

1 rosemary sprig, leaves stripped and chopped, plus 2 small sprigs to garnish

2–3 tablespoons crème fraîche or heavy cream

salt and black pepper

- Cook the parsnip and potatoes in a large saucepan of lightly salted boiling water for 15 minutes, until tender.

- Meanwhile, heat the oil in a large skillet, add the onion, and cook for 2–3 minutes, until starting to soften. Season the lamb and add to the skillet. Cook over high heat for 5 minutes, turning once, until browned and cooked to your liking. Remove from the skillet and keep warm.

- Add the wine, mustard, vinegar, and chopped rosemary to the skillet, bring to a boil, and simmer for a few minutes until slightly thickened. Return the lamb to the skillet and heat through, spooning the sauce over the lamb.

- Drain the vegetables, then return to the pan and mash with the crème fraîche or cream and plenty of black pepper. Serve the lamb and sauce on the mashed vegetables, garnished with the rosemary.

Stir-Fried Balsamic Lamb with Couscous

Place ¾ cup couscous in a heatproof bowl and cover with boiling water. Cover with plastic wrap and let stand for 5 minutes. Meanwhile, heat 1 tablespoon vegetable oil in a wok, add 10 oz boneless lamb cutlets, cut into strips, and stir-fry for 2 minutes, until browned. Add ½ teaspoon garlic paste, ¼ cup red wine, 1 teaspoon Dijon mustard, and 1 tablespoon balsamic vinegar and heat through, stirring, until bubbling. Fluff up the couscous with a fork, season, and stir in a little olive oil. Serve with the lamb and arugula leaves.

Balsamic Lamb with Rosemary Roasted Potatoes

Peel 1 parsnip and 3 russet potatoes, then cut into ½ inch pieces and place in a bowl. Toss with 2 tablespoons olive oil and 1 teaspoon chopped rosemary leaves and season. Transfer to a roasting pan and roast in a preheated oven, at 425°F, for 25 minutes, turning occasionally, until golden and tender. Meanwhile, heat 1 tablespoon olive oil in a skillet, add 2 seasoned lamb cutlets, about 5 oz each, and cook for about 5 minutes, turning once, until browned and cooked to your liking. Remove the lamb from the skillet. Add ½ cup red wine, 1 teaspoon Dijon mustard, and 2 tablespoons balsamic vinegar to the skillet and simmer until slightly thickened, then return the lamb and heat through in the sauce. Serve with the rosemary roasted potatoes.

 # Spicy Sausage and Arugula Pasta

Serves 4

8 oz penne or other pasta
2 tablespoons olive oil
8 Italian-style sausages, skins removed
1¾ cups tomato puree or tomato sauce
1 teaspoon dried red pepper flakes
4 handfuls of arugula leaves
salt and black pepper
grated Parmesan cheese, to serve

- Cook the penne in a large saucepan of lightly salted boiling water for about 10 minutes, or according to the package directions, until just tender.

- Meanwhile, heat the oil in a large skillet, break the sausages into small pieces, and add to the pan, then cook for 3–4 minutes, turning occasionally, until browned.

- Add the tomato puree or tomato sauce and chile flakes and season. Bring to a boil, then reduce the heat and simmer for 5 minutes, until the sauce is slightly reduced and the sausagemeat is cooked through.

- Drain the pasta, then add to the sauce and toss well to coat. Remove from the heat, stir in the arugula, and serve with grated Parmesan.

 Spicy Sausage and Arugula Baguettes Heat 2 tablespoons olive oil in a large skillet, add 8 Italian-style sausages, and cook for 8 minutes, until golden and cooked through. Split 4 small baguettes and spread each with 1 teaspoon basil pesto. Add the sausages, a handful of arugula leaves, and store-bought tomato salsa.

 Baked Spicy Sausage Pasta Cook 8 oz pasta in a large saucepan of lightly salted boiling water for about 10 minutes, or according to the package directions, until just tender. Meanwhile, remove the skins of 8 Italian-style sausages and break into pieces with your fingers. Heat 2 tablespoons olive oil in a large skillet, add the sausage pieces, and cook for 3–4 minutes, until golden. Add 1¾ cups tomato puree or tomato sauce and 1 teaspoon dried red pepper flakes and season. Bring to a boil, then reduce the heat and simmer for 5 minutes. Drain the pasta, then add to the sauce and toss well to coat. Transfer the mixture to a large ovenproof dish, then top with 8 oz sliced mozzarella cheese. Place in a preheated oven, at 400°F, for 10 minutes, until golden and bubbling. Serve with an arugula salad.

Lamb Meatballs with Herbed Feta Couscous

Serves 2

8 oz ground lean lamb
1 garlic clove, crushed
½ teaspoon ground cumin
½ teaspoon ground coriander
2 tablespoons olive oil
salt and black pepper
raita or Greek-style yogurt,
  to serve

For the couscous

¾ cup couscous
1 tablespoon chopped parsley
1 tablespoon chopped mint leaves
⅓ cup crumbled feta cheese
½ cup chopped store-bought
  cooked fresh beet

- Place the lamb in a bowl, add the garlic, cumin, and coriander, and season. Mix well, then, using your hands, shape into 8 meatballs, pressing the mixture together firmly.

- Heat the oil in a skillet, add the meatballs, and cook over medium heat for 8–10 minutes or until browned and cooked through.

- Meanwhile, place the couscous in a heatproof bowl and just cover with boiling water. Cover with plastic wrap and let stand for 5 minutes. Fluff up the couscous with a fork, then season and stir in the herbs. Lightly stir through the feta and beet.

- Serve the meatballs with the couscous and generous spoonfuls of raita or Greek yogurt.

---

10 **Lamb Burgers with Herb and Feta Couscous** Soak 1 (4½ oz) package of cilantro and lemon couscous in boiling water according to the package directions. Meanwhile, broil or grill 2 prepared lamb burgers, about 4 oz each, for about 5–8 minutes or until cooked through, turning once. Fluff up the couscous with a fork. Stir in ⅓ cup crumbled feta cheese and ½ cup chopped store-bought cooked fresh beet. Serve with the burgers.

30 **Moroccan Lamb Meatballs with Herbed Couscous** Put 8 oz ground lean lamb in a bowl, add 1 crushed garlic clove and 1 teaspoon ras el hanout (Moroccan spice blend), and season. Mix well and shape into 8 meatballs, pressing the mixture together firmly. Heat 1 tablespoon olive oil in a skillet, add the meatballs, and cook for 8–10 minutes, until golden. Add 1 (14½ oz) can diced tomatoes and bring to a boil, then reduce the heat and simmer for about 10 minutes. Meanwhile, put ¾ cup couscous in a heatproof bowl and just cover with boiling water. Cover with plastic wrap and let stand for 5 minutes. To make the raita, stir 1 tablespoon chopped mint leaves and 2 tablespoons coarsely grated cucumber into ¼ cup plain yogurt. Season with black pepper and set aside. Fluff up the couscous with a fork, then season and stir in 1 tablespoon each of chopped parsley and mint leaves. Serve the meatballs with the couscous and raita.

10 Eggs Benedict

Serves 2

2 extra-large eggs
2 English muffins
⅓ cup prepared Hollandaise sauce
2 thick slices of ham
salt and black pepper
chopped chives, to garnish
(optional)

- Break the eggs into a saucepan of simmering water and cook for 3–4 minutes for a soft yolk, or longer if you prefer your eggs completely set.

- Meanwhile, cut the muffins in half and toast them in a toaster or under a preheated broiler. Gently warm the Hollandaise sauce in a microwave-proof bowl in a microwave, in a double boiler, or in a heatproof bowl set over a saucepan of simmering water.

- Place the ham on one half of each muffin. Drain the eggs with a slotted spoon and place on the ham. Season, then spoon the warmed Hollandaise over the eggs and sprinkle with the chives, if using. Top with the remaining muffin halves and serve.

 Eggs Benedict with Homemade Hollandaise Sauce To make the sauce, whisk together 2 egg yolks, 1 teaspoon white wine vinegar, and 1 teaspoon lemon juice in a bowl. Gradually add 6 tablespoons butter, melted, whisking continuously. Season and add extra lemon juice to taste. Make the Eggs Benedict as above. Spoon the warmed Hollandaise sauce over the eggs and sprinkle with the chives.

 Poached Eggs on Ham Hash Browns Parboil 2 russet potatoes, peeled and halved, in a saucepan of lightly salted boiling water for 8–10 minutes. Drain and let cool slightly, then coarsely grate into a bowl. Add 2 slices of ham, finely chopped, and 2 chopped scallions. Season and mix lightly, then shape the mixture into 2 cakes. Heat 2 tablespoons olive oil in a skillet, add the cakes, and sauté over medium heat for 8–10 minutes, turning occasionally, until crisp and golden. In a separate saucepan, break 2 extra-large eggs into simmering water and poach for 3–4 minutes, or longer if you prefer a set yolk. Remove with a slotted spoon and serve on the hash browns with warmed prepared Hollandaise sauce spooned over the top. Sprinkle with chopped chives.

30 Pepperoni, Artichoke, and Olive Pizzas

Serves 2

all-purpose flour, for dusting
1 (6½ oz) package pizza crust mix
3 tablespoons tomato paste or
　sun-dried tomato pesto
4 oz artichoke antipasti from
　a jar, drained
3 oz sliced pepperoni
¼ cup pitted ripe black olives
4 oz mozzarella cheese, sliced
1 tablespoon olive oil
green salad, to serve

- Dust a large baking sheet with flour. Make up the pizza crust mix according to the package directions. Turn out the dough onto a lightly floured work surface and knead until smooth and stretchy, then cut in half and roll out 2 large circles. Place on the prepared baking sheet.

- Spread the tomato paste or pesto over the crusts, then top with the artichokes, pepperoni, and olives. Arrange the mozzarella on top and bake in a preheated oven, at 475°F, for 10–12 minutes or until the crusts are crisp and the topping is golden.

- Drizzle the oil over the pizzas and serve with a green salad.

 Pepperoni, Artichoke, and Olive Crostini Cut 1 small ciabatta loaf in half horizontally and place on a baking sheet. Drizzle 2 tablespoons garlic-infused olive oil over the slices and bake in a preheated oven, at 400°F, for 5 minutes, until crisp. Mix together 3 finely chopped tomatoes and 1 small finely chopped red onion in a bowl, then spoon the mixture over the bread. Top with 4 oz of artichoke antipasti from a jar, drained, 2 oz chopped pepperoni, and 8 pitted ripe black olives. Serve with a crisp green salad.

 Pepperoni, Artichoke, and Olive Tart Place ½ sheet of ready-to-bake puff pastry, thawed if frozen, on a baking sheet. Spread 2 tablespoons chili pesto over the pastry, leaving a ½ inch border around the edge. Top with 3 oz of artichoke antipasti from a jar, drained, 2 oz thinly sliced pepperoni, and 8 pitted ripe black olives. Bake in a preheated oven, at 400°F, for 15 minutes, or until the pastry is crisp and golden. Serve with an arugula and Parmesan salad.

Garlicky Pork with Warm Lima Bean Salad

Serves 4

¼ cup olive oil

2 garlic cloves, crushed

4 lean pork chops or cutlets, about 5 oz each

salt and black pepper

For the salad

2 tablespoons olive oil

2 (15 oz) cans lima beans, rinsed and drained

12 cherry tomatoes, halved

⅔ cup chicken stock

juice of 2 lemons

2 handfuls of parsley, chopped

- For the pork, mix together the oil and garlic in a bowl, then season. Place the pork on an aluminum foil-lined broiler rack and spoon the garlicky oil over the meat. Cook under a preheated medium broiler for about 10 minutes, turning occasionally, until golden and cooked through.

- Meanwhile, make the salad. Heat the oil in a large skillet, add the lima beans and tomatoes, and heat through for a few minutes. Add the chicken stock, lemon juice, and parsley and season. Serve with the broiled chops.

 Pork with Garlicky Mashed Lima Beans

Heat 2 tablespoons olive oil in a skillet, add 4 seasoned, thin pork cutlets, about 5 oz each, and cook for 5–6 minutes, turning occasionally, until cooked through and browned. Halfway through the cooking time, add 12 halved cherry tomatoes to the skillet and cook until softened, then stir in 2 handfuls of chopped parsley. Meanwhile, put 2 (15 oz) cans lima beans, rinsed and drained, ¼ cup garlic-infused olive oil, salt and black pepper, and a little water in a blender or food processor and process to form a smooth mash. Transfer to a microwave-proof bowl and heat in a microwave on High for 2 minutes, until hot. Serve the pork and pan juices with the mashed lima beans.

 Garlicky Pork and Lima Bean Stew

Heat 2 tablespoons olive oil in a large skillet, add 4 lean pork shoulder or loin cutlets, about 5 oz each and cut into chunks, and 2 chopped onions, and cook for a few minutes, stirring occasionally, until starting to brown. Add 2 crushed garlic cloves, 2 (15 oz) cans lima beans, rinsed and drained, 2 (14½ oz) cans diced tomatoes, and a dash of Worcestershire sauce and bring to a boil, then reduce the heat and simmer for 20 minutes, until the pork is cooked through. Season and stir in 2 handfuls of chopped parsley.

30 Creamy Peppered Steaks with Sweet Potato Fries

Serves 2

1 tablespoon black peppercorns, crushed

2 sirloin or tenderloin steaks, about 7 oz each

1 tablespoon olive oil

1 garlic clove, crushed

¼ cup crème fraîche or heavy cream

baby broccoli or green beans, to serve

For the fries

1 sweet potato, scrubbed and cut into fries

2 tablespoons olive oil

salt and black pepper

- Place the sweet potato in a bowl, toss with the oil and season, then spread over a baking sheet. Bake in a preheated oven, at 400°F, for 25 minutes, turning occasionally, until tender and golden.

- Meanwhile, spread the peppercorns over a plate and season with salt. Add the steaks and press the peppercorns firmly onto both sides.

- Heat a skillet or ridged grill pan until hot, drizzle the steaks with the oil, and cook for 3 minutes on each side for medium, or longer for well done. Remove from the pan, cover, and let rest.

- Add the garlic to the pan and cook for 1 minute, then stir in the crème fraîche or cream. Bring to a boil, stirring, adding a little water if the sauce is too thick. Spoon the sauce over the steaks and serve with the fries and broccoli or green beans.

---

10 Peppered Steak Wraps

Season both sides of 2 sirloin or tenderloin steaks, about 7 oz each, with plenty of coarsely ground black pepper and a little salt, pressing it on firmly, then cut into strips. Heat 1 tablespoon olive oil in a skillet, add the steak, and stir-fry over high heat for about 3 minutes. Pile onto 2 warm soft tortillas with mixed salad greens. Top with spoonfuls of sour cream mixed with creamed horseradish to taste. Roll up the tortillas and serve.

20 Peppered Steak Stroganoff

Season both sides of 2 sirloin or tenderloin steaks, about 7 oz each, with plenty of coarsely ground black pepper and a little salt, pressing it on firmly, then cut into strips. Cook 6 oz tagliatelle or pappardelle in a saucepan of lightly salted boiling water for about 10 minutes, or according to the package directions, until just tender. Meanwhile, heat 2 tablespoons olive oil in a wok or skillet, add the steak strips, and stir-fry over high heat for about 3 minutes. Add 2 cups sliced mushrooms and cook for 1 minute, then stir in 1 crushed garlic clove, ¼ cup crème fraîche or heavy cream, 1 teaspoon Dijon mustard, and 1 teaspoon tomato paste. Bring to a boil, stirring, adding a little water if the sauce is too thick. Drain the pasta and serve with the stroganoff.

30 Lamb and Chorizo Burgers with Roasted New Potatoes

Serves 4

1 lb ground lean lamb

8 oz cooking chorizo, skin removed

1 garlic clove, crushed

2 tablespoons chopped parsley

2 tablespoons olive oil

4 slices of ciabatta bread, toasted

¼ cup fresh prepared tomato salsa

For the potatoes

1¼ lb new potatoes, halved if large

2 tablespoons olive oil

2 rosemary sprigs, leaves stripped and coarsely chopped

salt and black pepper

- Place the potatoes in a large roasting pan and drizzle with the oil, then add the rosemary and season. Roast in a preheated oven, at 400°F, for 25 minutes, until tender and golden.

- Meanwhile, place the lamb in a bowl and crumble in the chorizo. Add the garlic and parsley and mix well. Using your hands, shape into 4 large patties, pressing the mixture together firmly.

- Heat the oil in a large skillet or ridged grill pan, add the patties, and cook over medium heat for 10 minutes, turning occasionally, until browned and cooked through.

- Place the burgers on the toasted ciabatta slices and top each with a spoonful of salsa. Serve with the roasted new potatoes.

---

10 Quick Lamb Burgers with Chorizo

Cook 4 prepared lamb burgers, about 4 oz each, on an aluminum foil-lined broiler rack under a preheated hot broiler for 5–8 minutes, turning once, until cooked through. At the same time, broil 12 thin slices of chorizo until crisp. Top each burger with 3 slices of the chorizo, 2 slices of tomato, and 2 slices of mozzarella cheese. Return to the broiler and cook for 1 minute, until the cheese starts to melt. Serve on toasted burger buns with salad greens and prepared tomato salsa.

20 Chorizo-Topped Lamb with Spicy

Fries Sprinkle 2 teaspoons Cajun seasoning over 1 lb frozen prepared oven fries and cook in a preheated oven, at 425°F, for 15–20 minutes, until crisp and golden. Meanwhile, heat a large skillet or ridged grill pan until hot, add 8 oz sliced chorizo sausage, and cook for 2 minutes, until crisp and browned. Remove from the skillet and set aside. Add 4 seasoned lamb cutlets, about 5 oz each, to the chorizo fat in the skillet and cook for 6–8 minutes, turning once, until browned and cooked to your liking. Remove the lamb from the skillet and keep warm. Stir a dash of red wine vinegar into the pan juices with the juice of 2 lemons. Return the chorizo to the pan and simmer for 1 minute. Pour the chorizo and juices over the lamb cutlets and serve with the fries and fresh tomato salsa.

30 Prosciutto and Asparagus Tart

Serves 2

8 asparagus spears, trimmed
½ sheet of ready-to-bake
   puff pastry
1 tablespoon pesto sauce
2 oz thinly sliced prosciutto
4 cherry tomatoes, halved
salt

To serve

Parmesan cheese shavings
arugula leaves
balsamic syrup

- Cook the asparagus in a saucepan of lightly salted boiling water for 2 minutes. Drain and rinse under cold water, then drain again.

- Place the pastry on a baking sheet. Spread the pesto sauce evenly over the pastry, leaving a ½ inch border around the edge. Arrange the asparagus on the pesto. Ruffle up the prosciutto and place on top with the tomatoes.

- Bake in a preheated oven, at 400°F, for 15–20 minutes, until the pastry is crisp and golden. Serve warm with Parmesan cheese shavings, arugula leaves, and a drizzle of balsamic syrup.

 Crispy Prosciutto and Chargrilled Asparagus Salad Heat a ridged grill pan or skillet until hot. Toss 12 trimmed asparagus spears with 1 tablespoon olive oil in a bowl, then season. Add to the pan with 2 oz ruffled slices of prosciutto and cook for 5–6 minutes, until the asparagus is tender and the ham is crisp. Serve the asparagus and prosciutto with a peppery mix of salad greens, halved cherry tomatoes, a drizzle of balsamic syrup, and warm ciabatta bread.

 Prosciutto and Asparagus Pizza Spread 1 tablespoon pesto sauce over a store-bought 9 inch pizza crust. Top with 8 trimmed thin asparagus spears, 2 oz ruffled slices of prosciutto, and 4 halved cherry tomatoes. Sprinkle with ¼ cup grated Parmesan cheese and bake in a preheated oven, at 400°F, for 15 minutes, until crisp and golden. Serve in wedges with arugula leaves and a drizzle of balsamic syrup.

Grilled Lamb Cutlets and Tomatoes with Mashed Beans

Serves 4

8 lamb cutlets

2 tablespoons olive oil

2 pinches of smoked paprika

1 garlic clove, crushed

2 teaspoons finely chopped
rosemary leaves

20 cherry tomatoes on the vine

For the mashed beans

⅓ cup olive oil

1 red chile, seeded and halved

2 tablespoons rosemary leaves

2 (15 oz) cans cannellini beans,
rinsed and drained

¾ cup hot chicken stock

- Place the lamb, oil, paprika, garlic, and rosemary in a large bowl and toss well. Let marinate.

- Meanwhile, make the mashed beans. Heat the oil in a large skillet, add the chile and rosemary, and cook for 2 minutes, then remove the chile and rosemary with a slotted spoon.

- Return the skillet to the heat, add the beans, and cook for 1 minute, then pour in the stock and bring to a boil. Reduce the heat and simmer for 5 minutes, until slightly reduced. Transfer to a food processor and process until almost smooth, retaining a little texture. Set aside and keep warm.

- Heat a large ridged grill pan until smoking, add the lamb, and cook over high heat for 4–5 minutes, turning once, until browned all over and cooked to your liking, adding the tomatoes around the edges for the final 2 minutes. Serve with the mashed beans.

 Lamb, Tomato, and Bean Pan-Fry

Heat ¼ cup olive oil in a large skillet, add 1 lb thinly sliced boneless shoulder of lamb and 2 thinly sliced red onions, and cook over high heat for 4 minutes, until golden. Add 2 (15 oz) cans cannellini beans, rinsed and drained, 2½ cups halved cherry tomatoes, and 2 tablespoons chopped rosemary leaves, and stir-fry for 2–3 minutes, until piping hot, then add 1¼ cups boiling chicken stock. Serve with crusty bread.

 Roasted Lamb with Beans and Tomatoes Put 2 (10 oz) lamb mini roasts in a large roasting pan, then rub each with 1 crushed garlic clove and sprinkle with 1 tablespoon chopped rosemary leaves. Roast in a preheated oven, at 425°F, for 10 minutes. Mix together 2 (15 oz) cans cannellini beans, rinsed and drained, 1¼ cups hot chicken stock, and 3 cups halved cherry tomatoes and pour around the lamb, then return to the oven and cook for another 15 minutes or until the lamb roasts are cooked through but still slightly pink in the center. Slice and serve with the beans and tomatoes.

30 Tex-Mex Pork Ribs with Corn and Red Pepper Salsa

Serves 2

3 tablespoons ketchup

2 tablespoons packed brown sugar

2 tablespoons honey

1 tablespoon Worcestershire sauce

1 lb rack of mini pork ribs

For the salsa

1 (11 oz) can corn kernels, drained

1 red bell pepper, cored, seeded, and thinly sliced

1 bunch of scallions, finely chopped

¼ cup chopped parsley

2 tablespoons olive oil

black pepper

- Mix together the ketchup, sugar, honey, and Worcestershire sauce in a small bowl, then brush all over the ribs. Place the ribs in a large baking dish and bake in a preheated oven, at 425°F, for 25 minutes, until browned and cooked through.

- Meanwhile, make the salsa. Mix together all the ingredients in a bowl and season well with black pepper.

- Cut the pork into separate ribs and serve with the corn and red pepper salsa.

 Pork, Corn, and Red Pepper

Stir-Fry Heat 1 tablespoon sesame oil in a wok, add 8 oz thinly sliced pork tenderloin and 1 cored, seeded, and thinly sliced red bell pepper, and stir-fry over high heat for 4 minutes. Add 1½ cups frozen corn kernels and 1 bunch of scallions, finely chopped, and cook for 2 minutes, stirring occasionally. Meanwhile, mix together 3 tablespoons ketchup, 1 tablespoon packed brown sugar, and 1 tablespoon soy sauce. Pour in, toss, and cook until piping hot. Serve with cooked rice, if desired.

 Red Pepper Pork with Creamed Corn

Make a large slit lengthwise down the side of 2 boneless pork cutlets to form pockets. Heat 1 tablespoon olive oil in a skillet, add 1 cored, seeded, and thinly sliced red bell pepper, and cook over high heat for 3–4 minutes, adding 4 finely sliced scallions for the final 2 minutes. Stir in 2 tablespoons chopped parsley. Remove from the heat, then stuff the mixture into the pork pockets. Lightly brush with olive oil and season well. Cook under a preheated hot broiler for 3–4 minutes on each side, or until browned and cooked through. Meanwhile, put 1 (8¼ oz) can cream-style corn kernels in a saucepan and heat gently for 2–3 minutes, until hot, then stir in 3 tablespoons chopped parsley. Serve the pork with the creamed corn.

 Caramelized Bacon and Pine Nut Parsnips

Serves 2

4 parsnips, scrubbed or peeled
4 tablespoons butter
6 oz bacon, diced
3 tablespoons sugar
⅓ cup pine nuts
⅓ cup chopped thyme leaves

- Cut the parsnips in half widthwise, then cut the chunky tops into quarters lengthwise and the slim bottom halves in half lengthwise.

- Heat the butter in a large skillet or wok, add the bacon and parsnips, and cook over medium heat for 15 minutes, turning and tossing occasionally, until the parsnips are golden and softened and the bacon is crisp.

- Add the sugar and pine nuts and cook for another 2–3 minutes, until lightly caramelized. Toss with the thyme and serve.

 Bacon, Pine Nut, and Parsnip Cakes

Grate 3 peeled parsnips into a bowl and mix with 2 oz store-bought cooked bacon strips, snipped into small pieces, and 2 tablespoons chopped parsley. Squeeze the mixture together into 4 balls, then flatten into patties. Heat 4 tablespoons butter in a large skillet, add the patties, and cook over high heat for 2 minutes on each side until browned. Serve hot, sprinkled with pine nuts, with salad.

 Bacon, Pine Nut, and Parsnip Gratin

Heat 4 tablespoons butter in a large skillet, add 4 peeled and thickly sliced parsnips and 6 oz bacon, cut into small pieces, and cook for 15 minutes, until golden. Add 1 (15 oz) jar fresh cheese sauce and ⅓ cup chopped parsley and stir together. Transfer to a large, shallow gratin dish and sprinkle with ⅓ cup fresh bread crumbs and 3 tablespoons grated Parmesan cheese. Cook under a preheated broiler for 5 minutes, until the sauce is bubbling and the bread crumbs are golden. Sprinkle with 2 tablespoons toasted pine nuts and 3 tablespoons chopped thyme leaves and serve.

30 Moroccan Lamb Kebabs with Warm Chickpea Salad

Serves 2

12 oz shoulder of lamb, cubed

2 teaspoons harissa paste

1 teaspoon ground cumin

1 teaspoon ground coriander

For the chickpea salad

2 tablespoons olive oil

1 large red onion, sliced

1 tablespoon cumin seeds

½ red chile, seeded and thinly sliced

1 (15 oz) can chickpeas, rinsed and drained

¼ tablespoons chopped cilantro leaves

1 tablespoon water

2 cups arugula leaves

salt and black pepper

- Place the lamb, harissa, and ground spices in a bowl and toss well to coat. Thread onto 4 presoaked wooden skewers or metal ones and set aside.

- To make the chickpea salad, heat the oil in a large skillet, add the onion, and cook over medium heat for 5 minutes, until slightly browned and softened. Add the cumin seeds and chile and cook for 1 minute. Add the chickpeas and cook for another 2 minutes, then add the chopped cilantro. Season well and set aside.

- Cook the kebabs under a preheated hot broiler for about 8–10 minutes, turning once, until browned and cooked through. Return the chickpeas to the heat, add the measured water, and then toss with the arugula.

- Spoon the chickpeas onto 2 warm serving plates and top with the lamb kebabs. Serve hot.

 Harissa Lamb Pita Breads with Hummus Heat 1 tablespoon olive oil in a skillet, add 8 oz thinly sliced shoulder of lamb, and cook over high heat for 2–3 minutes. Add 1 tablespoon harissa paste and cook, stirring, for 1 minute. Remove from the heat and stir in 2 tablespoons chopped parsley. Fill 2 pita breads with salad greens and top with the lamb, then spoon over store-bought hummus and sprinkle with 6 halved cherry tomatoes. Serve hot.

 One-Pan Harissa Lamb and Chickpeas Heat 1 tablespoon olive oil in a large wok or skillet, add 12 oz cubed shoulder of lamb and 1 chopped onion, and cook over high heat for 3–4 minutes, until browned. Add 2 tablespoons harissa paste and 1 (14½ oz) can diced tomatoes. Bring to a boil, then add 1 (15 oz) can chickpeas, rinsed and drained. Cook for another 3–4 minutes, until the sauce is slightly reduced, then stir in ¼ cup chopped cilantro leaves.

Serve hot with warm crusty bread, if desired.

Spiced Beef and Onion Chapattis

Serves 2

10 oz top sirloin steak, thinly
  sliced
1 small onion, thinly sliced
1 teaspoon ground cumin
½ teaspoon ground paprika
½ teaspoon ground coriander
2 tablespoons olive oil
1 red onion, cut into slim wedges
2 soft wheat chapattis
2 tablespoons Indian-style relish
2 handfuls of salad greens
salt and black pepper

- Put the steak, sliced onion, spices, and 1 tablespoon of the oil in a bowl and toss well to coat, then season.

- Heat the remaining oil in a skillet, add the red onion wedges, and cook over medium heat for 2–3 minutes, until softened. Add the steak and sliced onion and cook for 1–2 minutes on each side, until browned and cooked through.

- Warm the chapattis according to the package directions. Spoon the beef and onions onto one side of each and top with the Indian-style relish and salad greens, then fold over to enclose the filling and serve.

Spicy Beef Rolls with Onions

Put 2 thin top sirloin steaks, about 5 oz each, between 2 sheets of lightly oiled plastic wrap and bash with a rolling pin until almost twice the size and half the thickness. Remove the plastic wrap and lightly spread each steak with 1 tablespoon Indian-style relish and season. Sprinkle each with 1 tablespoon chopped cilantro leaves, then roll up tightly and secure with toothpicks. Heat 1 tablespoon olive oil in a skillet, add the steak rolls and 1 thinly sliced onion, and cook for 5 minutes, stirring and turning frequently, until browned. Serve sprinkled with extra chopped cilantro.

Spiced Beef and Onion Curry

Heat 2 tablespoons olive oil in a large skillet, add 10 oz cubed top sirloin steak and 1 large chopped onion, and cook over high heat for 5 minutes. Add 1 tablespoon ground cumin, 1 tablespoon ground coriander, and 2 teaspoons mild chili powder and cook for 1 minute. Add 1 (14½ oz) can diced tomatoes and 1¼ cups hot beef stock and bring to a boil, then reduce the heat, cover, and simmer over low heat for 15 minutes. Blend 1 tablespoon cornstarch with 2 tablespoons water, then add to the skillet and stir until thickened. Stir in ¼ cup chopped cilantro leaves, then serve with warm chapattis and an Indian-style relish.

Creamy Pork, Apple, and Mustard Pan-Fry

Serves 4

2 tablespoons olive oil

2 tablespoons butter

1 large red onion, cut into
thin wedges

2 crisp red apples, cored and
cut into thin wedges

1¼ lb pork tenderloin, thinly sliced

1¼ cups hot chicken stock

1 cup crème fraîche or
heavy cream

2 tablespoons Dijon mustard

2 tablespoons whole-grain
mustard

⅓ cup chopped parsley

mashed potatoes or crusty bread,
to serve (optional)

- Heat the oil and butter in a large skillet, add the onion and apples, and cook over medium-high heat for 5 minutes, turning and stirring occasionally, until golden and starting to soften. Remove with a slotted spoon and keep warm.

- Add the pork to the skillet and cook over high heat for 5 minutes, until browned and cooked through. Return the onion and apples to the skillet with the stock and bring to a boil. Reduce the heat and simmer for 3 minutes, until the stock has reduced by half, then add the crème fraîche or cream and mustards and heat through for 2 minutes.

- Stir in the parsley, then serve hot with mashed potatoes or crusty bread, if desired.

Simple Pork, Apple, and Mustard

Pan-Fry Heat 2 tablespoons olive oil and 2 tablespoons butter in a large skillet, add 1 large cored and coarsely chopped apple and 1¼ lb thinly sliced pork tenderloin, and cook for 5 minutes, stirring occasionally, until browned and cooked through. Stir in 1 cup crème fraîche or heavy cream and 2 tablespoons whole-grain mustard until well combined. Sprinkle with 2 tablespoons chopped parsley and serve with cooked rice or mashed potatoes, if desired.

Pork, Apple, and Mustard Gratins

Heat 2 tablespoons olive oil in a large skillet, add 2 thinly sliced red onions, 2 cored and coarsely chopped crisp red apples, and 1¼ lb thinly sliced pork tenderloin, and cook for 8–10 minutes, until golden and softened. Add 1¼ cups hot chicken stock and bring to a boil, then reduce the heat and simmer for 2 minutes, until reduced by half. Stir in 1 cup crème fraîche or heavy cream and 2 tablespoons Dijon mustard, then divide among 4 small gratin dishes. Remove the crusts from 4 slices of wheat bread and put into a food processor, then process briefly to form chunky bread crumbs. Transfer to a bowl and mix in ½ cup grated Parmesan cheese and 2 tablespoons chopped parsley. Sprinkle evenly over the tops of the gratin dishes, then cook under a preheated broiler for 3–4 minutes, until browned and bubbling. Serve with green vegetables or salad, if desired.

30 Sausages in Red Wine with Creamy Layered Potatoes

Serves 2

1 tablespoon olive oil
6 Italian-style sausages
1 large red onion, thinly sliced
1 tablespoon juniper berries,
 lightly crushed
⅔ cup red wine
1¼ cup hot beef stock
1 teaspoon cornstarch
1 tablespoon water
salt and black pepper
chopped parsley, to garnish

For the potatoes

3 red-skinned or white round
 potatoes, peeled and sliced
⅔ cup heavy cream
2 tablespoons grated Parmesan
 cheese

- Heat the oil in a skillet, add the sausages, onion, and juniper berries and cook over medium heat for 10–12 minutes, stirring occasionally, until cooked through.

- Pour in the red wine and stock, increase the heat, and bring to a boil. Season well, then reduce the heat and simmer for about 5 minutes, stirring occasionally, until reduced by about one-third. Blend the cornstarch with the water, then add to the skillet and stir briskly until the sauce is thickened.

- Meanwhile, cook the potatoes in a saucepan of lightly salted boiling water for 8 minutes, until tender but not losing their shape. Drain, then return to the pan, toss with the cream, and season well. Transfer to a shallow gratin dish and sprinkle with the Parmesan. Cook under a preheated medium-hot broiler for about 8–10 minutes or until bubbling. Serve with the sausages, sprinkled with parsley.

---

10 Sausage Ball and Red Wine Pan-Fry

Using your hands, shape 10 oz sausagemeat into 12 balls. Heat 1 tablespoon olive oil in a large skillet, add the balls, and cook for 4 minutes, turning occasionally, until golden. Add 1 teaspoon lightly crushed juniper berries and cook for 1 minute, then stir in 1¼ cups prepared red wine cooking sauce (see right) and heat through for 3 minutes. Sprinkle with 2 tablespoons chopped thyme leaves and serve with cooked mashed potatoes, if desired.

20 Sausages in Red Wine Gravy with Cheesy Potatoes

Cook 2 large baking potatoes in a microwave on High for 10 minutes or until cooked. Meanwhile, heat 1 tablespoon olive oil in a skillet, add 4 Italian-style sausages and 1 thinly sliced red onion, and cook over medium heat for 10 minutes, turning the sausages occasionally, until cooked through. Add ⅔ cup red wine and ⅔ cup hot chicken stock and bring to a boil, then reduce the heat and simmer for 5 minutes, until reduced by half.

Stir in 2 tablespoons thyme leaves and season well with black pepper. When the potatoes are cooked, remove from the microwave and cut in half. Mash the insides a little with a fork and season well, then drizzle 1 tablespoon heavy cream and sprinkle 1 tablespoon grated Parmesan cheese over each. Cook under a preheated broiler for 3–5 minutes, until browned and bubbling. Serve the cheesy potatoes with the sausages.

10 Warm Prosciutto, Chicken Liver, and Walnut Salad

Serves 2

3 tablespoons olive oil

3 oz prosciutto, torn into big pieces

12 oz chicken livers, drained and halved

⅔ cup walnut pieces

1 bunch of watercress

handful of arugula leaves

3 tablespoons balsamic vinegar

crusty bread, to serve (optional)

- Heat 1 tablespoon of the oil in a large skillet, add the prosciutto, and cook over high heat for 2 minutes, until crisp and browned, turning once. Remove from the skillet and place in a large, heatproof salad bowl.

- Add the chicken livers and walnuts to the skillet and cook over high heat for 3–4 minutes, until browned and the chicken livers are cooked through, but still slightly pink in the center. Add to the prosciutto and toss in the watercress and arugula.

- In a small bowl, whisk together the vinegar and remaining oil, then pour the dressing over the salad and toss well to lightly coat. Serve warm with crusty bread, if desired.

 Chicken Livers in Prosciutto with Walnut Salad Drain 12 oz chicken livers, then tightly wrap each with ½ slice of prosciutto and secure with toothpicks. Put on an aluminum foil-lined broiler rack and cook under a preheated hot broiler for 5–7 minutes, turning once, until browned and cooked through. Meanwhile, toss 2 bunches of watercress with 2 tablespoons each of olive oil and balsamic vinegar, and ⅓ cup coarsely chopped walnut pieces, then divide between 2 serving plates. Remove the toothpicks and put the chicken livers in a bowl, then toss with 1 tablespoon honey and 1 teaspoon whole-grain mustard. Serve the salad topped with the chicken livers.

 Prosciutto, Chicken Liver, and Walnut Sauce Put 4 peeled, coarsely chopped carrots, 1 coarsely chopped onion, and 2 cups coarsely chopped mushrooms in a food processor and process until finely chopped. Heat ¼ cup olive oil in a skillet, add the vegetables, and cook for 4 minutes. Add 4 oz drained and coarsely chopped chicken livers and 2 finely chopped slices of prosciutto and cook, stirring, for 5 minutes, until cooked through. Add 3 tablespoons coarsely chopped walnuts and cook for another 1 minute, then add ⅔ cup red wine and bring to a boil. Reduce the heat, cover, and simmer for 10 minutes, until soft. Serve with pasta.

3 Pan-Fried Liver with Caper Sauce and Mashed Vegetables

Serves 2

1 tablespoon olive oil
1 small onion, sliced into rings
1 lb liver, cut into strips
1 tablespoon all-purpose flour
2 tablespoons capers, drained and
   coarsely chopped
⅔ cup heavy cream
1 teaspoon Dijon mustard
salt and black pepper

For the mashed vegetables

2 russet or Yukon gold potatoes,
   peeled and cubed
4 carrots, peeled and cubed
1 large parsnip, peeled and cut
   into chunks
2 tablespoons butter

- Cook the root vegetables in a large saucepan of lightly salted boiling water for 20 minutes, until tender.

- Meanwhile, heat the oil in a skillet, add the onion, and cook over low heat for 3 minutes, until softened. Remove from the skillet and keep warm.

- Place the liver on a plate and lightly sprinkle with the flour, then season on each side. Add to the hot pan and cook for 3 minutes on each side until golden brown and cooked through. Remove from the skillet and keep warm.

- Return the onion to the skillet with the capers, cream, and mustard and gently stir until hot but not boiling.

- Drain the vegetables, return to the pan, and, using a potato masher, mash well with the butter. Season well with black pepper and spoon onto 2 warm serving plates. Add the liver and sauce and serve.

 Quick Liver and Capers

Toss 8 oz drained and thinly sliced liver in 1 tablespoon seasoned all-purpose flour mixed with ½ teaspoon dry mustard. Heat 2 tablespoons olive oil in a skillet, add 1 thinly sliced onion, and cook, stirring, over medium heat for 2 minutes, then add the liver and cook for 4–5 minutes, until cooked through. Add 1 tablespoon drained capers and ⅔ cup heavy cream and bring to a boil. Serve with cooked mashed potatoes.

 Pan-Fried Liver and Capers with Sautéed Parsnips Heat 2 tablespoons olive oil and 1 tablespoon butter in a large skillet, add 3 peeled and thinly sliced parsnips, and cook over medium heat for 6–7 minutes, until golden and cooked through. Remove with a slotted spoon and keep warm. Meanwhile, heat another 1 tablespoon olive oil in the skillet. Toss 8 oz thinly sliced liver in 1 tablespoon seasoned all-purpose flour and cook in the hot oil for 2 minutes, then add 1 thinly sliced red onion and cook for another 3–4 minutes, until softened and browned and the meat is cooked through. Add 1 tablespoon drained capers and ⅔ cup heavy cream and toss and stir for 2 minutes, until piping hot. Serve with the parsnips.

30 Spicy Sausage, Rosemary, and Bean Stew

Serves 4

12 Italian-style pork sausages
2 tablespoons olive oil
1 large red onion, cut into thin wedges
2 tablespoons rosemary leaves
1 small mild red chile, seeded and thinly sliced
4 tomatoes, coarsely chopped
2 (15 oz) cans lima beans, rinsed and drained
1 (15 oz) can great Northern beans, rinsed and drained
2½ cups tomato puree or tomato sauce
warm crusty bread, to serve

- Cook the sausages under a preheated hot broiler for 8–10 minutes, turning occasionally, until cooked through.

- Meanwhile, heat the oil in a large saucepan, add the onion, and cook over medium heat for 3–4 minutes, until slightly softened, then add the rosemary and chile and cook for another 2 minutes. Add the tomatoes and cook for 3 minutes, stirring occasionally, then add the beans and tomato puree or tomato sauce and bring to a boil.

- Reduce the heat, add the sausages, cover, and simmer for 15 minutes, stirring occasionally, until piping hot and the sauce is thick, adding a little water, if necessary. Serve with warm crusty bread.

---

1 **Spicy Sausage and Rosemary Sandwiches** Heat 2 tablespoons olive oil in a large skillet, add 8 good-quality link sausages, 1 large thinly sliced red onion, and 2 tablespoons rosemary leaves and cook for 8–10 minutes, turning frequently, until browned and cooked through. Cut 4 small, slim French bread rolls in half. Spread the top half of each with 1 tablespoon chili relish, then fill each with 2 sausages, onions, and rosemary and top with a handful of arugula leaves.

2 **Spicy Sausage, Rosemary, and Bean Pan-Fry** Cook 12 good-quality sausages under a preheated hot broiler for 10 minutes, until cooked through, turning occasionally. Remove from the broiler and slice thickly. Meanwhile, heat 2 tablespoons olive oil in a large skillet, add 2 thinly sliced onions, and cook for 3–4 minutes, then add 2 tablespoons chopped rosemary leaves and 2 teaspoons dried red pepper flakes. Add the sausages and 2 (15 oz) cans great Northern beans, rinsed and drained, and 1¾ cups tomato puree or tomato sauce. Bring to a boil, then reduce the heat and simmer for 10 minutes. Serve with warm crusty bread.

3⏱ Beef, Squash, and Prune Stew

Serves 4

2 tablespoons olive oil
1 garlic clove, chopped
1 large onion, chopped
½ peeled, seeded, and cubed
    butternut squash or 4 cups
    peeled, seeded, and cubed
    pumpkin
1¼ lb top sirloin or tenderloin
    steak, cubed
2 teaspoons ground coriander
2 teaspoons ground cumin
15 soft dried pitted prunes
2 (14½ oz) cans diced tomatoes
2 cups hot beef stock
2½ cups chopped cilantro leaves

To serve
couscous (optional)
plain yogurt

- Heat the oil in a large saucepan or flameproof casserole, add the garlic, onion, butternut squash or pumpkin, and beef and cook over high heat for 5–10 minutes, until the beef is browned and the squash is golden. Add the spices and cook for another 1 minute.

- Add the prunes, tomatoes, and stock and bring to a boil, then reduce the heat, cover, and simmer for 15 minutes, stirring occasionally, until the stew is thickened and the meat and vegetables are cooked through.

- Sprinkle with the chopped cilantro and stir through. Serve with couscous, if desired, topped with spoonfuls of yogurt.

 Speedy Beef, Tomato, and Prune Pan-Fry Heat 2 tablespoons olive oil in a large skillet, add 1¼ lb thinly sliced top sirloin or tenderloin steak, and cook over high heat for 2 minutes. Add 2 teaspoons ground coriander, 2 teaspoons ground cumin, and 8 chopped tomatoes and cook for another 2–3 minutes, until softened. Serve hot, sprinkled with 12 coarsely chopped dried pitted prunes and 2 tablespoons chopped cilantro leaves.

 Beef, Squash, and Prune Soup Heat 2 tablespoons olive oil in a large saucepan, add ½, peeled, seeded, and cubed butternut squash or 4 cups peeled, seeded, and cubed pumpkin and 2 tablespoons ground coriander and cook for 5 minutes, stirring occasionally, until softened. Add 2 (14½ oz) cans diced tomatoes and 2 cups hot beef stock and bring to a boil, then reduce the heat, cover, and simmer for 8 minutes, until tender. Meanwhile, heat 2 tablespoons olive oil in a large skillet, add 12 oz finely diced top sirloin or tenderloin steak, and cook over high heat for 3–4 minutes, until browned and cooked. Remove from the heat and set aside. Put the squash mixture into a food processor and process until smooth. Return to the heat and add the chopped steak and 8 coarsely chopped dried pitted prunes. Serve sprinkled with chopped cilantro leaves.

30 Risotto-Topped Lamb and Vegetable Casserole

Serves 2

1 cup risotto rice
2 tablespoons olive oil
2 zucchini, coarsely chopped
1 small eggplant, coarsely chopped
10 oz ground lamb
2 tomatoes, coarsely chopped
1 (14½ oz) can diced tomatoes
1 egg
1 cup shredded cheddar cheese
salt and black pepper
arugula salad, to serve (optional)

- Cook the rice in a saucepan of lightly salted boiling water for 20 minutes, or according to the package directions, until tender.

- Meanwhile, heat the oil in a large skillet, add the zucchini and eggplant, and cook over high heat for 5 minutes, then add the lamb and cook for another 10 minutes, until the meat is browned.

- Add the fresh tomatoes and cook, stirring, for 2 minutes, then add the canned tomatoes and bring to a boil. Reduce the heat, cover, and simmer for 5 minutes.

- Drain the rice and place in a bowl, then mix in the egg and two-thirds of the cheese. Season well.

- Spoon the lamb and vegetables into a shallow gratin dish, then spoon the rice mixture over the top. Sprinkle with the remaining cheese. Cook under a preheated hot broiler for 2–3 minutes, until golden. Serve hot with a arugula salad, if desired.

 Lamb and Vegetable Pilaf

Heat 2 tablespoons olive oil in a large saucepan, add 8 oz thinly sliced shoulder of lamb and 2 small halved and thinly sliced zucchini, and cook over high heat for 5 minutes, until cooked through. Add 4 coarsely chopped tomatoes and cook for another 2 minutes, then add a 2 cups cooked rice and cook for 5 minutes, until piping hot. Season well and serve.

 Lamb and Vegetable Risotto

Heat 1 tablespoon olive oil in a large skillet, add 1 coarsely chopped onion, and cook for 2 minutes, then add 1 cup risotto rice and 2½ cups hot rich chicken stock and bring to a boil. Reduce the heat, cover, and simmer over low heat for 15 minutes, stirring occasionally, until tender. Meanwhile, heat 1 tablespoon olive oil in a separate skillet, add 6 oz ground lamb and 1 coarsely chopped zucchini, and cook for 10 minutes, until browned and cooked through, adding 2 coarsely chopped tomatoes for the final 2–3 minutes. Once the rice is tender and cooked, stir in the lamb and vegetables. Season well and serve.

 # Steaks with Easy Braised Red Cabbage and Blackberries

Serves 2

2 tenderloin steaks, about
   5 oz each
1 tablespoon butter
salt and black pepper
mashed potatoes, to serve
   (optional)

For the red cabbage

2 tablespoons olive oil
1 red onion, thinly sliced
½ red cabbage, thinly shredded
3 tablespoons balsamic vinegar
¼ cup firmly packed brown sugar
1 teaspoon allspice
2 tablespoons red currant jelly
1 cup blackberries

- To make the red cabbage, heat the oil in a saucepan, add the onion, and cook over medium heat for 3 minutes, then add the red cabbage and cook for another 3 minutes, stirring continuously.

- Add the vinegar, sugar, and allspice, cover, and cook over low heat for 10 minutes, until the cabbage is soft and tender, adding the red currant jelly and blackberries for the final 3 minutes.

- Meanwhile, season the steaks well. Heat the butter in a skillet, add the steaks, and cook over high heat for 2–3 minutes on each side until browned and cooked to your liking.

- Spoon the red cabbage onto 2 warm serving plates and top with the steaks. Serve with mashed potatoes, if desired.

---

1 0 **Steaks with Blackberry Sauce and Red Cabbage** Heat 2 tablespoons butter in a large skillet, add ¼ finely shredded red cabbage, 1 teaspoon lightly crushed juniper berries, and ½ teaspoon allspice and cook over medium heat for 5 minutes. In a separate skillet, heat 1 tablespoon butter and cook 2 thin 4 oz seasoned tenderloin or top sirloin steaks to your liking, turning halfway through cooking. Add ½ cup blackberries and ⅓ cup red currant jelly and stir until melted. Serve the steaks with the red cabbage, with the sauce spooned over the top.

3 0 **Beef, Blackberry, and Red Cabbage Stew** Heat 2 tablespoons olive oil in a large saucepan, add 10 oz cubed top sirloin or tenderloin steak, and cook for 2 minutes, then add 1 sliced red onion, 2 teaspoons lightly crushed juniper berries, 1 teaspoon ground allspice, and ¼ shredded red cabbage and cook for another 5 minutes. Add 1 raw beet, peeled and cut into thin wedges, and cook for 1 minute. Add 1¼ cups hot beef stock and ⅔ cup red wine and bring to a boil. Reduce the heat, cover, and simmer gently for 15 minutes, then add 1 cup blackberries.

Cook for another 3–4 minutes, until the blackberries have just lost their shape. Blend 1 teaspoon cornstarch with 1 tablespoon water, then add to the pan and stir until thickened. Serve with crusty wheat bread to mop up the juices.

10 Chorizo and Ham Eggs

Serves 2

1 tablespoon olive oil
1 small red pepper, cored, seeded, and sliced
4 oz thinly sliced chorizo
2 tomatoes, coarsely chopped
2 oz wafer-thin ham
2 handfuls of baby spinach leaves
2 extra-large eggs
warm crusty bread, to serve

- Heat the oil in a skillet, add the red bell pepper and chorizo, and cook over high heat for 2 minutes, until lightly browned. Add the tomatoes and cook for another 2 minutes, then add the ham and spinach and cook, stirring occasionally, for 2 minutes.

- Divide the mixture between 2 small, individual pans, if you have them (if not, continue to cook in one pan). Make wells in the tomato mixture and break the eggs into the wells. Cook over medium heat for 2–3 minutes, until set. Serve with warm crusty bread to mop up the juices.

 Chorizo and Ham Tortilla

Heat 3 tablespoons olive oil in a large, flameproof skillet, add 4 oz thickly sliced chorizo, 1 sliced red onion, and ½ cored, seeded, and thinly sliced red bell pepper and cook for 5 minutes, until softened, then add 2 oz wafer-thin ham, torn into small pieces. In a small bowl, whisk together 5 eggs with plenty of salt and black pepper. Add a large handful of spinach leaves to the skillet and stir for 2 minutes, until wilted. Pour in the eggs and cook over low heat until the bottom is set. Place the skillet under a preheated hot broiler and cook the tortilla for 3–4 minutes, until the top is firm and set. Serve cut into wedges.

 Baked Eggs with Chorizo and Ham

Heat 2 tablespoons olive oil in a skillet, add 4 oz coarsely diced chorizo and ½ cored, seeded, and diced red bell pepper, and cook for 5 minutes, until lightly browned and softened. Lightly grease 2 ramekin dishes and break 2 eggs into each. Mix 2 tablespoons chopped parsley and 1 oz wafer-thin ham, shredded, into the chorizo mixture and sprinkle with the eggs, then season well. Place in a roasting pan and pour in enough boiling water to come halfway up the sides of the dishes. Bake in a preheated oven, at 400°F, for 20 minutes, until firm and set. Serve with wilted spinach and crusty bread.

QuickCook
Chicken

Recipes listed by cooking time

30

20

10

3 ⏱ Chicken and Sweet Potato Curry

Serves 4

2 tablespoons vegetable oil

1 large onion, chopped

1 medium red chile, seeded
and chopped

1 lb boneless, skinless chicken
breasts, chopped

4 sweet potatoes, peeled and
cut into chunks

2–4 tablespoons korma
curry paste

1¾ cups can coconut milk

1 (14½ oz) can diced tomatoes

2½ cups trimmed and halved
green beans

2 tablespoons chopped cilantro
leaves

boiled basmati rice or other
long-grain rice, to serve

- Heat the oil in a large saucepan, add the onion, and cook for 2–3 minutes, until softened. Add the chile, chicken, and sweet potatoes and cook for 5 minutes, stirring occasionally.

- Add the korma paste and cook for 1 minute, then add the coconut milk, tomatoes, and green beans. Bring to a boil, then reduce the heat, cover, and simmer for 15 minutes, until the sweet potato is tender and the chicken is cooked through.

- Stir the cilantro into the boiled basmati or other long-grain rice and serve with the curry.

---

1 ⏱ Chicken, Spinach, and Potato Curry

Heat 2 tablespoons vegetable oil in a large skillet, add 1 lb chicken strips and cook over high heat for 2 minutes, until golden. Add 2 tablespoons curry paste and ⅓ cup water. Heat for 1 minute, then stir in 1 (10 oz) package fresh spinach and 2 peeled, cubed, and cooked red-skinned or white round potatoes. Cook for 5 minutes, stirring occasionally, until piping hot and the chicken is cooked through. Serve with naan.

2 ⏱ Chicken, Potato, and Pea Curry

Heat ¼ cup vegetable oil in a large saucepan, add 1 lb chicken strips, and stir-fry over high heat for 2 minutes, until golden. Add 1 teaspoon garlic paste and 2–4 tablespoons curry paste. Cook for 1 minute, then add 1¾ cups coconut milk and 1 (14½ oz) can diced tomatoes. Stir in 1½ (14½ oz) cans sliced new potatoes, drained, and 1⅔ cups frozen peas. Bring to a boil, then reduce the heat, cover, and simmer for about 10 minutes, until cooked through. Stir in 2 tablespoons chopped cilantro leaves and serve with boiled basmati rice or other long-grain rice.

Chicken and Dolcelatte Pasta Casserole

Serves 2

2 tablespoons olive oil
1 small onion, chopped
6 oz skinless chicken breast, chopped
⅔ cup heavy cream
⅓ cup dry white wine
1 teaspoon whole-grain mustard
6 oz pasta, such as penne
2 cups broccoli florets
3 oz dolcelatte cheese, chopped
½ cup fresh bread crumbs
salt and black pepper
green salad, to serve

- Heat 1 tablespoon of the oil in a skillet, add the onion, and cook for 2 minutes, then add the chicken and cook for another 5 minutes, until cooked through. Stir in the cream, wine, and mustard and simmer for 5 minutes.

- Meanwhile, cook the pasta in a saucepan of lightly salted boiling water for 10 minutes, or according to the package directions, until just tender, adding the broccoli for the final 5 minutes. Drain, add to the sauce, and stir well to coat. Add the cheese, stir well, and season.

- Transfer the mixture to an ovenproof dish, sprinkle with the bread crumbs, and drizzle over the remaining oil. Bake in a preheated oven, at 400°F, for 15 minutes, until golden and bubbling. Serve with a green salad.

 Chicken and Dolcelatte Tagliatelle Heat 1 tablespoon olive oil in a skillet, add 6 oz chicken strips, and sauté for 2 minutes, until browned. Add ⅔ cup heavy cream, ⅓ cup dry white wine, and 1 teaspoon whole-grain mustard and simmer for 5 minutes, until the chicken is cooked through. Meanwhile, cook 8 oz fresh egg tagliatelle and ½ cup frozen peas in a saucepan of lightly salted boiling water for 3 minutes or until just tender. Add 3 oz chopped dolcelatte cheese to the sauce and stir until melted, then season. Drain the tagliatelle, add to the sauce, and lightly stir to coat.

 Chicken and Dolcelatte Pasta Gratin Cook 6 oz pasta, such as penne, in a large saucepan of lightly salted boiling water for 10 minutes, or according to the package directions, until just tender, adding 2 cups frozen broccoli florets for the final 5 minutes. Meanwhile, heat 1 tablespoon olive oil in a skillet, add 6 oz chicken strips, and sauté for 2 minutes, until browned. Add ⅔ cup heavy cream, ⅓ cup dry white wine, and 1 teaspoon whole-grain mustard and simmer for 5 minutes, until the chicken is cooked through. Drain the pasta and broccoli, add to the sauce, and toss well to coat. Stir in 3 oz chopped dolcelatte cheese, season, and transfer to a flameproof dish. Sprinkle with 2 tablespoons grated Parmesan cheese and cook under a preheated medium broiler for 5 minutes, until golden.

30 Chicken Parmigiana

Serves 2

¼ cup olive oil

1 small eggplant, sliced

1 garlic clove, crushed

1¼ cups tomato puree or
tomato sauce

1 tablespoon chopped fresh
oregano, plus extra to garnish

2 tablespoons all-purpose flour

1 egg, beaten

1½ cups fresh white bread crumbs

2 small skinless chicken breasts,
about 5 oz each, halved
horizontally

4 oz mozzarella cheese, sliced

salt and black pepper

spaghetti, to serve

- Heat 2 tablespoons of the oil in a large, flameproof skillet, add the eggplant slices, and sauté for 1 minute on each side. Add the garlic, tomato puree or tomato sauce, and oregano and season. Bring to a boil, then reduce the heat, cover, and simmer for 10 minutes, stirring occasionally.

- Meanwhile, place the flour, beaten egg, and bread crumbs on separate plates. Dip the chicken pieces in the flour, shaking off any excess, then coat in the egg and finally the bread crumbs, pressing them on firmly.

- Heat the remaining oil in a large skillet, add the coated chicken, and cook for about 5 minutes on each side, until golden brown and cooked through. Place on top of the eggplant sauce and top with the mozzarella.

- Place the skillet under a preheated medium broiler for 3–4 minutes, until the cheese is melted. Garnish with oregano and serve with spaghetti.

 Easy Chicken Parmigiana

Heat 2 tablespoons olive oil in a large, flameproof skillet, add 10 oz store-bought breaded chicken strips, and sauté for 8 minutes, turning occasionally, until browned and cooked through. Meanwhile, heat 1⅓ cups tomato sauce in a saucepan until hot. Pour the sauce over the chicken and top with 4 oz sliced mozzarella cheese. Place the skillet under a preheated medium broiler for 2 minutes, until the cheese is melted. Serve with a green salad.

 Chicken in Cheesy Eggplant and Tomato Sauce Cut 2 small boneless, skinless chicken breasts, about 5 oz each, in half horizontally. Heat 2 tablespoons olive oil in a large, flameproof skillet, add the chicken, and sauté for 2–3 minutes on each side until browned. Add 1 small eggplant, cut into chunks, and cook for 2 minutes, until golden, adding an extra tablespoon of oil, if needed. Stir in 1 crushed garlic clove, 1¼ cups tomato puree or tomato sauce, and 1 tablespoon chopped fresh oregano or ½ teaspoon dried oregano and season. Cover and simmer for 10 minutes, until cooked through. Remove the lid and arrange 4 oz sliced mozzarella cheese over the top. Place the skillet under a preheated medium broiler for 2 minutes, until the cheese is melted. Serve with spaghetti.

30 Roasted Lemon Chicken with Zucchini

Serves 2

4 chicken thighs, about 4 oz each
finely grated rind of 1 lemon
1 garlic clove, crushed, plus
  2 whole cloves, unpeeled
¼ cup olive oil
12 oz new potatoes, halved
  if large
1 red onion, cut into wedges
1 zucchini, thickly sliced
1 tablespoon thyme leaves, plus
  a few sprigs to garnish
salt and black pepper

- Cut a few slashes across each chicken thigh. Mix together the lemon rind, crushed garlic, and 2 tablespoons of the oil in a bowl, then rub the mixture over the chicken, pushing it into the slashes. Place in a roasting pan with the potatoes and season. Roast in a preheated oven, at 425°F, for 10 minutes.

- Add the onion, zucchini, unpeeled garlic, and thyme leaves to the pan and drizzle with the remaining oil. Return to the oven and roast for another 15 minutes or until the chicken is golden and cooked through and the vegetables are tender.

- Squeeze the soft garlic over the chicken and vegetables, discarding the skin, and serve garnished with thyme sprigs.

 Lemon Chicken and Zucchini Stir-Fry

Heat 1 tablespoon vegetable oil in a wok or large skillet, add 8 oz chicken strips, and stir-fry over high heat for 2 minutes, until browned. Add 1 chopped zucchini and 4 chopped scallions and stir-fry for another 2 minutes, until the vegetables are just tender and the chicken is cooked through. Stir in 1 (4 oz) envelope lemon stir-fry sauce. Heat through, then stir in the leaves from 1 head of bok choy and cook until just wilted. Serve with cooked rice.

 Lemon Chicken and Zucchini Risotto

Heat 1 tablespoon olive oil in a skillet, add 6 oz chopped, skinless chicken breast and 1 crushed garlic clove, and sauté for 2 minutes, until browned. Add 1 chopped zucchini and sauté for another 2 minutes, then stir in ½ (6 oz) package asparagus-flavored instant risotto rice. Cook for 12 minutes, or according to the package directions, until the rice is creamy and the chicken is cooked through. Stir in 1 teaspoon finely grated lemon rind and season to taste. Serve sprinkled with grated Parmesan cheese.

20 Thai Chicken and Vegetable Kebab Wraps

Serves 4

2 tablespoons Thai red curry paste
juice of 2 limes
¼ cup plain yogurt, plus extra
  to serve
2 tablespoons coconut milk
12 oz skinless chicken breasts,
  cut into chunks
1 red bell pepper, cored, seeded,
  and cut into chunks
1 large zucchini, thickly sliced
2 tablespoons olive oil
4 large soft tortilla wraps
½ cucumber, cut into sticks
2 handfuls of bean sprouts
sweet chili sauce, to serve

- Mix together the curry paste, lime juice, yogurt, and coconut milk in a large, nonmetallic bowl. Add the chicken and stir well to coat. Let marinate for 5 minutes.

- Thread the chicken pieces onto 8 metal skewers, alternating them with the red bell pepper and zucchini. Drizzle with the oil and cook under a preheated medium broiler for 8–10 minutes, turning occasionally, until the chicken is cooked through and just starting to char and the vegetables are tender.

- Meanwhile, warm the tortillas in a microwave. Divide the cucumber and bean sprouts among the wraps, top with the chicken and vegetables, and add a dash of sweet chili sauce and a spoonful of yogurt to each. Roll up the tortilla wraps and serve.

10 Thai Chicken and Vegetable Noodles

Heat 2 tablespoons vegetable oil in a wok, add 1 lb chicken strips, and stir-fry over high heat for 2 minutes, until browned. Add 1–2 tablespoons Thai red curry paste and the juice of 2 limes and stir-fry for 1 minute, then stir in 1 (1 lb) package prepared stir-fried vegetables and cook for another 2 minutes, until the vegetables are just tender and the chicken is cooked through. Add 1½ (7 oz) pouches cooked noodles and heat through, stirring, then add a dash of soy sauce and sweet chili sauce and serve.

30 Thai Chicken with Vegetable Rice

Cut a few slashes across 4 boneless, skinless chicken breasts, about 5 oz each. Mix together 2 tablespoons Thai red curry paste, the juice of 2 limes and ½ cup plain yogurt in a large nonmetallic dish. Add the chicken and turn to coat. Let marinate for 10 minutes. Heat 2 tablespoons vegetable oil in a large skillet, add 2 crushed garlic cloves, 2 cored, seeded, and chopped red bell peppers, and 2 chopped zucchini and sauté for 2–3 minutes. Stir in 1½ cups jasmine rice and coat in the oil.

Add 2½ cups hot chicken stock and bring to a boil, then reduce the heat, cover, and simmer for 10 minutes, until the stock has been absorbed and the rice is tender. Stir in 2 tablespoons chopped cilantro leaves. Meanwhile, cook the chicken on an aluminum foil-lined broiler rack under a preheated medium broiler for 10–15 minutes, turning occasionally, until cooked through and just starting to char at the edges. Serve the chicken with the rice, extra yogurt, and a drizzle of sweet chili sauce.

 # Chicken and Corn Chowder

Serves 2

2 tablespoons butter

1 large Yukon gold, white round, or red-skinned potato, peeled and cut into small chunks

2 scallions, chopped

2 bacon strips, chopped

5 oz skinless chicken breast, chopped

⅔ cup hot chicken stock

1 (10½ oz) can condensed mushroom soup

1 cup milk

½ cup frozen or canned corn kernels

1 tablespoon chopped parsley

salt and black pepper

crusty bread, to serve

- Heat the butter in a saucepan, add the potatoes, scallions, bacon, and chicken, and sauté for 5 minutes, stirring. Pour in the stock and simmer for 5 minutes, until the potatoes are tender and the chicken is cooked through.

- Add the soup, milk, and corn kernels and bring to a boil, stirring, then reduce the heat, cover, and simmer for 5 minutes. Season and add the parsley. Serve with crusty bread.

 Quick Chicken and Corn Soup

Heat 1 tablespoon butter in a saucepan, add 5 oz chopped skinless chicken breast, 2 chopped bacon strips, and 2 chopped scallions, and cook for 5 minutes, stirring, until the chicken and bacon are cooked through. Add 2½ cups creamy vegetable soup and ½ cup frozen or canned corn kernels and heat through for about 4–5 minutes, until piping hot. Sprinkle with chopped parsley and serve with crusty bread.

Creamy Chicken and Corn Chowder

Heat 2 tablespoons butter in a saucepan, add 1 chopped onion, 2 chopped bacon strips, 1 large Yukon gold, white round, or red-skinned potato, peeled and chopped, and 1 celery stick, chopped, and cook for 5 minutes. Pour in 2 cups hot chicken stock and add 1 cup frozen or canned corn kernels and 1 whole boneless, skinless chicken breast, about 5 oz. Bring to a boil, then reduce the heat, cover, and simmer for 10 minutes, until the vegetables are tender and the chicken is cooked through. Remove the chicken from the pan and set aside. Blend the soup with an immersion blender until creamy but still with some vegetable pieces. Chop the chicken and return to the pan, then add 1 tablespoon chopped parsley and ¼ cup light cream. Season and heat through. Serve with garlic bread.

 # Paprika Chicken Quesadillas

Serves 2

1 tablespoon olive oil

1 teaspoon smoked paprika

1 garlic clove, crushed

12 oz chicken strips

2 soft flour tortillas, halved

1 cup shredded cheddar cheese

2 tablespoons sliced jalapeño
  peppers from a jar

2 tablespoons cilantro leaves

store-bought fresh tomato salsa,
  to serve

- Heat the oil, paprika, and garlic in a skillet, add the chicken, and cook over medium heat for 5 minutes, until the chicken is cooked through. Remove from the skillet, then wipe the pan clean with paper towels.

- Place the tortillas on a board and cover one half of each tortilla with cheese, cooked chicken, jalapeño peppers, and cilantro. Fold each tortilla to enclose the filling.

- Heat the skillet until hot, add the tortilla sandwiches, and cook for 2 minutes on each side, until crisp and the cheese starts to melt.

- Serve the quesadillas, cut into wedges, with tomato salsa.

 Grilled Chicken Tortillas

Place 2 soft flour tortillas on a board. Sprinkle with 1 cup shredded cheddar cheese, top with 4 oz store-bought cooked chicken, sliced, and a few teaspoons of store-bought spicy tomato salsa. Cover with 2 more tortillas. Cook in a hot skillet, one tortilla sandwich at a time, for 2 minutes on each side, until hot. Cut into wedges and serve with extra salsa and sour cream.

 Smoky Chicken Quesadillas with Corn Salsa To make the salsa, mix together 1 cup canned corn kernels, 1 chopped scallion, 1 tablespoon chopped cilantro leaves, and 1 tablespoon sweet chili sauce. Set aside. Mix together ½ teaspoon smoked paprika and ½ teaspoon Cajun seasoning in a bowl, add 5 oz chicken strips, and toss well to coat. Heat 1 tablespoon olive oil in a skillet, add the chicken, and cook for 5 minutes, until cooked through. Remove from the skillet, then wipe the pan clean. Sprinkle 1 cup shredded cheddar cheese over 2 soft flour tortillas, then top with the cooked chicken, 2 tablespoons sliced jalapeño peppers from a jar, and 2 tablespoons cilantro leaves. Cover with 2 more tortillas. Cook the tortilla sandwiches in the skillet, one at a time, for 2–3 minutes on each side. Cut into wedges and serve with the salsa.

30 Sticky Soy Chicken with Fruity Asian Salad

Serves 4

2 tablespoons honey

3 tablespoons ketchup

2 tablespoons vegetable oil

2 tablespoons soy sauce

2 teaspoons sweet chili sauce

8 chicken thighs, about
   3–4 oz each

For the salad

2 Boston lettuce, shredded

1 red onion, thinly sliced

8 radishes, sliced

1 orange, peel and with pith
   removed, halved and sliced

2 tablespoons soy sauce

¼ cup orange juice

2 tablespoons olive oil

- Mix together the honey, ketchup, vegetable oil, soy sauce, and sweet chili sauce in a large bowl. Cut a few slashes across each chicken thigh and coat in the honey mixture. Place in an aluminum foil-lined roasting pan and cook in a preheated oven, at 400°F, for 25 minutes or until cooked through.

- Meanwhile, to make the salad, place the lettuce leaves in a salad bowl with the onion, radishes, and orange slices. Mix together the soy sauce, orange juice, and olive oil in a bowl, then pour over the salad. Serve with the chicken.

---

1  **Spicy Chicken with Soy and Pineapple Noodles** Heat 2½ lb cooked, spicy chicken wings in a microwave according to the package directions. Meanwhile, cook 10 oz medium egg noodles in a saucepan of lightly salted boiling water for 3 minutes, or according to the package directions, then drain and toss with 4 drained canned pineapple slices, chopped, 2 tablespoons soy sauce, 4 teaspoons sesame seeds, and 4 thinly sliced scallions. Serve with the chicken wings and Chinese plum sauce for dipping.

2 **Sticky Soy Chicken and Pineapple Skewers** Mix together 2 tablespoons honey, 3 tablespoons ketchup, 2 tablespoons vegetable oil, ¼ cup soy sauce, and 2 teaspoons sweet chili sauce in a large bowl. Add 12 oz skinless chicken breasts, cut into bite-size chunks, and stir well to coat. Thread the chicken onto 8 metal skewers, alternating with chunks of fresh or canned pineapple. Cook on an aluminum foil-lined broiler rack under a preheated medium broiler for about 10 minutes, turning occasionally, until the chicken is cooked through and lightly charred. Meanwhile, cook 1 (8 oz) pouch of flavored rice according to the package directions. Serve with the chicken skewers, sprinkled with strips of scallion.

MID-CHIC-DYH

30 Caribbean Chicken with Rice and Peas

Serves 2

2 teaspoons jerk seasoning

1 teaspoon peeled and grated
fresh ginger root

juice of 1 lime

2 boneless, skinless chicken
breasts, about 5 oz each

3 tablespoons vegetable oil

1 small onion, chopped

1 garlic clove, crushed

¾ cup long-grain rice

¾ cup hot chicken stock

¾ cup coconut milk

¾ cup rinsed and drained,
canned red kidney beans

⅓ cup frozen or canned
corn kernels

few thyme sprigs, plus extra
to garnish

lime wedges, to serve

- Mix together the jerk seasoning, ginger, and lime juice in a nonmetallic bowl. Cut a few slashes across each chicken breast and coat in the mixture. Heat 2 tablespoons of the oil in a skillet, add the chicken, and cook over medium heat for 15–20 minutes, turning occasionally, until cooked through.

- Meanwhile, heat the remaining oil in a saucepan, add the onion and garlic, and cook for 2 minutes, until slightly softened. Add the rice, stock, and coconut milk and bring to a boil, then reduce the heat, cover, and simmer for 15–20 minutes, until the liquid has been absorbed and the rice is tender, adding the kidney beans, corn, and thyme sprigs for the final 5 minutes.

- Slice the chicken and serve with the rice and lime wedges, garnished with a few sprigs of thyme.

10 Quick Caribbean Chicken

Heat 1 tablespoon oil in a skillet, add 8 oz chicken strips, and stir-fry over high heat for 2–3 minutes or until golden. Reduce the heat and stir in 3 tablespoons jerk barbecue sauce and the juice of 1 lime. Add 2 cups cooked rice, ¾ cup rinsed and drained, canned kidney beans, and ⅓ cup canned or frozen corn kernels and heat through until piping hot. Serve sprinkled with thyme leaves.

20 Caribbean Chicken, Rice, and Pea Stew

Heat 1 tablespoon vegetable oil in a saucepan, add 1 chopped onion, 1 crushed garlic clove, and 4 chopped boneless, skinless chicken thighs (about 4 oz each) and cook for 3–4 minutes. Add 2 teaspoons jerk seasoning, ¾ cup long-grain rice, ¾ cup canned diced tomatoes, 1¼ cups hot chicken stock, and 2 tablespoons jerk barbecue sauce. Bring to a boil, then reduce the heat, cover, and simmer for 15 minutes, until the rice and chicken are cooked and the liquid has been absorbed, adding ¾ cup canned kidney beans and ⅓ cup frozen or canned corn kernels for the final 5 minutes. Serve sprinkled with thyme leaves.

 # Mexican Chicken Burgers with Tomato Salad

Serves 2

2 boneless, skinless chicken breasts, about 5 oz each, halved horizontally
2 teaspoons fajita seasoning
1 tablespoon olive oil
1 red bell pepper, cored, quartered, and seeded
2 soft hamburger buns, halved
½ avocado, peeled, pitted, and sliced
2 tablespoons sour cream
chopped chives

For the tomato salad

5 cherry tomatoes, halved
½ small red onion, thinly sliced
½ red chile, seeded and chopped
1 tablespoon chopped flat-leaf parsley
squeeze of lime juice
salt and black pepper

- Coat the chicken pieces in fajita seasoning, place on an aluminum foil-lined broiler rack, and drizzle with the oil, then add the bell pepper quarters, skin side up, to the broiler rack. Cook under a preheated medium broiler for 10–15 minutes, turning occasionally, until the chicken is cooked through and the bell peppers are soft and lightly charred.

- Meanwhile, make the salad. Mix together all the ingredients in a bowl and season.

- Mix together the sour cream and chives in a small bowl.

- Toast the buns. Then fill with avocado slices, the chicken, and the broiled bell peppers. Top with spoonfuls of tomato salad and sour cream. Serve with the remaining salad.

 ### Loaded Chicken Nachos

Spread out 7 oz tortilla chips in an ovenproof dish. Sprinkle with 1 cup chopped, cooked barbecue chicken. Top with 2 tablespoons tomato salsa. Add 1 tablespoon sliced jalapeño peppers from a jar and sprinkle with ¾ cup shredded cheddar cheese. Cook under a preheated hot broiler for 3–4 minutes, until melted and warm. Serve with store-bought guacamole.

 ### Mexican Roasted Chicken Tortillas

Place 2 boneless, skinless chicken breasts, about 5 oz each and each cut into 3 pieces, in a roasting pan with 1 red onion, cut into wedges, and 1 red bell pepper, cored, seeded, and cut into chunks. Drizzle with 2 tablespoons olive oil and season. Roast in a preheated oven, at 425°F, for 20 minutes, until cooked through and starting to char. Meanwhile, peel, pit, and mash 1 small ripe avocado. Stir in ½ seeded and chopped red chile and season with lime juice and salt. Set aside. Pour 1 cup fajita cooking sauce from a jar over the chicken and turn to coat in the sauce. Return to the oven and cook for another 5 minutes, until heated through. Serve with the avocado on warm tortillas with sour cream.

10 Lemon and Parsley Chicken Skewers

Serves 2

10 oz skinless chicken breasts, cut into chunks
finely grated rind and juice of 1 lemon
2 tablespoons olive oil
3 tablespoons finely chopped parsley
salt and black pepper

To serve
arugula and tomato salad
warm pita breads
1 cup prepared riata, Greek yogurt, or sour cream dip

- Place the chicken in a nonmetallic bowl with the lemon rind and juice and the oil and toss well to coat. Stir in the parsley and season well.

- Thread the chicken onto 4 small metal skewers and cook under a preheated hot broiler for 6–7 minutes, until golden and cooked through, turning once. Serve with a simple arugula and tomato salad, warm pita breads, and spoonfuls of riata, yogurt, or sour cream dip.

 2 Lemon and Parsley-Stuffed Chicken Make a slit lengthwise in the side of 2 boneless chicken breasts, about 5 oz each, to form pockets. Thinly slice ½ lemon, then stuff the chicken with the lemon slices. Press a small bunch of parsley into the cavities and season. Tie around each piece once with a piece of kitchen string. Heat 2 tablespoons butter and 1 tablespoon olive oil in a skillet, add the chicken, and cook over medium-high heat for 5–6 minutes on each side ,until browned and cooked through. Serve with Greek yogurt and a simple salad.

 3 Baked Lemon and Parsley Chicken Place 4 chicken thighs, about 4 oz each, and 1 large coarsely chopped zucchini in a small roasting pan, sprinkle with 2 tablespoons chopped parsley, and season well. Squeeze the juice of ½ lemon over the top, then cut the remaining lemon half into wedges and sprinkle around the chicken. Drizzle with 2 tablespoons olive oil, then bake in a preheated oven, at 400°F, for 20–25 minutes or until golden and cooked through. Meanwhile, mix together ⅓ cup heavy cream and 2 tablespoons plain yogurt, then place in a saucepan with 2 tablespoons chopped mint leaves. Heat for 2 minutes, until warm but not boiling. Serve the chicken and zucchini with the sauce spooned over the top.

Creamy Chicken and Tarragon Pasta

Serves 4

8 oz penne
¼ cup olive oil
1 lb skinless chicken breasts,
  cut into thin strips
3 zucchini, cut into thin slices
1 large onion, thinly sliced
2 teaspoons crushed garlic
¼ cup pine nuts
finely grated rind and juice of
  2 lemons
½ cup chopped tarragon
1 cup crème fraîche or
  heavy cream
salt

To serve

grated Parmesan cheese
simple salad (optional)

- Cook the penne in a large saucepan of lightly salted boiling water for 8–10 minutes, or according to the package directions, until just tender.

- Meanwhile, heat the oil in a large skillet and cook the chicken for 3–4 minutes, until starting to turn brown. Add the zucchini and onion and cook for another 5 minutes, until browned and the chicken is cooked through.

- Add the garlic and pine nuts and cook, stirring, for 2 minutes, then add the lemon rind and juice, tarragon, and crème fraîche or heavy cream and stir well until hot but not boiling.

- Drain the pasta well, then add to the sauce and toss well to coat. Serve with grated Parmesan and a simple salad, if desired.

 Creamy Chicken and Tarragon Pan-Fry Heat 2 tablespoons olive oil in a large skillet, add 2 thinly sliced onions and 1 lb thinly sliced skinless chicken breasts, and cook for 5 minutes, until browned and cooked through. Add ¼ cup chopped tarragon and 2 tablespoons white wine vinegar and cook for another 1 minute, then stir in 1 cup crème fraîche or heavy cream and 2 teaspoons Dijon mustard. Serve hot.

 Baked Chicken with Creamy Tarragon Sauce Make a slit lengthwise in the side of 4 boneless chicken breasts, about 5 oz each, with the skin still on. Open up and season well, then fill each with 2 tarragon sprigs and close up. Place in a large roasting pan with 3 thickly sliced zucchini and roast in a preheated oven, at 425°F, for 25 minutes or until cooked through. Meanwhile, heat 2 tablespoons olive oil in a skillet, add 4 finely chopped small shallots, and cook for 3–4 minutes, until softened. Add ¼ cup chopped tarragon and 2 tablespoons white wine vinegar and cook for a few seconds, then stir in 1 cup crème fraîche or heavy cream and 2 teaspoons Dijon mustard and heat through for 1 minute. Serve the chicken with the sauce spooned over the top.

30 Greek Chicken Stifado

Serves 2

3 tablespoons olive oil
2 chicken quarters
2 shallots, peeled and cut in half
1 fennel bulb, trimmed and cut
into thin wedges
1 (14 oz) can artichokes,
drained and halved
½ cup pitted kalamata olives
3 tablespoons tomato paste
2 tomatoes, coarsely chopped
1 tablespoon rosemary leaves
1¼ cups hot chicken stock
warm crusty bread, to serve
(optional)

- Heat the oil in a large skillet, add the chicken, skin side down, shallots, and fennel wedges and cook over medium-high heat for 10 minutes, until the chicken is browned.

- Turn the chicken over and add the artichokes, olives, tomato paste, tomatoes, rosemary, and stock and stir well, then cover tightly and simmer for 15–20 minutes, until the chicken is cooked through and the tomatoes have softened, adding a little water if the sauce is too thick. Serve with warm crusty bread, if desired, to mop up the juices.

10 Chicken, Artichoke, and Olive Pan-Fry

Heat 2 tablespoons olive oil in a large skillet, add 10 oz thinly sliced, skinless chicken breasts, and cook over high heat until browned, then add 1 teaspoon rosemary leaves, 1 (14 oz) can artichokes, drained, ¾ cup pitted ripe black olives, and 1¼ cups tomato sauce with vegetables from a jar and cook for 5 minutes, until piping hot and the chicken is cooked through. Serve with cooked rice or warm crusty bread to mop up the juices.

20 Chicken, Artichoke, and Olive Pasta

Heat 2 tablespoons olive oil in a large skillet, add 1 trimmed and finely sliced fennel bulb and 10 oz thinly sliced skinless chicken breasts, and cook for 5 minutes, until the fennel is softened and the chicken is cooked through. Add ⅓ cup tomato paste, 1 (14 oz) can artichokes, drained and halved, ¾ cup pitted ripe black olives, and ⅔ cup water, and bring to a boil, stirring, then reduce the heat, cover, and simmer for 5 minutes. Meanwhile, cook 8 oz penne in a saucepan of lightly salted boiling water for 8–10 minutes, or according to the package directions, until just tender. Drain the pasta well, then add to the sauce and stir well to coat. Serve with plenty of grated Parmesan cheese.

30 Thyme-Roasted Chicken and Carrots

Serves 4

8 chicken thighs, about
   3½–4 oz each
2 large red onions, cut into
   wedges
2 lemons, cut into wedges
12 oz baby carrots
¼ cup olive oil
⅓ cup balsamic vinegar
⅓ cup thyme leaves
1¼ cups hot chicken stock
black pepper
crusty bread or mashed potatoes,
   to serve

- Place the chicken thighs, onions, lemon wedges, carrots, oil, vinegar, and thyme in a large bowl and toss together with plenty of black pepper. Transfer to a large, shallow baking dish and roast in a preheated oven, at 425°F, for 15 minutes.

- Pour in the stock, then return to the oven and cook for another 10 minutes or until the chicken is browned and cooked through. Serve with warm crusty bread to mop up the juices, or mashed potatoes, if desired.

 Pan-Fried Chicken, Carrots, and Thyme
Heat 4 tablespoons butter in a large skillet, add 1 lb halved baby carrots and 1 lb thinly sliced skinless chicken breasts, and cook over medium heat for 5 minutes, until the chicken is cooked through and the carrots are just tender, then add 1¼ cups hot chicken stock, ¼ cup thyme leaves, and 2 tablespoons whole-grain mustard and cook for another 2 minutes. Serve with warm crusty bread.

 Sticky Chicken and Carrots with Thyme Heat 4 tablespoons butter and 2 tablespoons olive oil in a large skillet, add 2 thinly sliced, large red onions and 1 lb thinly sliced skinless chicken breasts, and cook for about 8–10 minutes, until browned and softened. Meanwhile, cook 1 lb baby carrots, halved lengthwise, in a large saucepan of boiling water for 5 minutes, until just tender. Drain well and add to the chicken with ¼ cup balsamic vinegar, then stir and cook gently for another 5 minutes, until the chicken and carrots are cooked through, adding ¼ cup chopped thyme leaves for the final 1 minute. Serve hot.

1 Chicken and Chorizo with Green Lentils

Serves 2

1 tablespoon olive oil
1 small onion, thinly sliced
4 oz chorizo sausage, thinly sliced
10 oz skinless chicken breasts, cubed
1¼ cups cooked green lentils
2 tablespoons thyme leaves
⅔ cup hot chicken stock
1 tablespoon Dijon mustard
salt and black pepper
crusty bread, to serve (optional)

- Heat the oil in a large skillet, add the onion, chorizo, and chicken, and cook over medium-high heat for 5–7 minutes, stirring occasionally, until browned and the chicken is cooked through.

- Add the lentils, thyme, stock, and mustard and stir well to combine, then cook for another 2 minutes, until boiling. Season well with black pepper and a little salt to taste. Serve with crusty bread, if desired.

2 Chicken and Chorizo Kebabs

with Lentil Puree Thread 4 oz thickly sliced chorizo sausage, 8 oz cubed skinless chicken breasts, and 1 onion, cut into wedges, onto 4 metal skewers. Brush with 1 tablespoon olive oil and season. Cook under a preheated medium broiler for 8–10 minutes, turning frequently, until cooked through. Meanwhile, put 1¼ cups cooked green lentils and ⅓ cup hot chicken stock in a saucepan and bring to a boil. Add 1 tablespoon thyme leaves and season, then transfer to a food processor and process until smooth. Serve with the kebabs.

3 Chicken, Chorizo, and Lentil Soup

Heat 1 tablespoon olive oil in a large saucepan, add 1 coarsely chopped onion, 4 oz diced chorizo sausage, and 5 oz coarsely diced, skinless chicken breast, and cook for 4–5 minutes, until browned and the chicken is cooked through. Add 1 cup green lentils and 2 cups hot chicken stock and bring to a boil. Reduce the heat, cover, and simmer for 20 minutes, until the lentils are tender. Stir in 1 tablespoon Dijon mustard and season well. Transfer the mixture to a food processor and process until almost smooth. Serve with crusty bread.

20 Chicken, Pancetta, and Mushroom Carbonara

Serves 2

8 oz linguine
2 tablespoons olive oil
10 oz skinless chicken breasts, cut into chunks
2 cups quartered cremini mushrooms
4 oz pancetta, cut into small pieces
2 egg yolks
1¼ cups heavy cream
½ cup grated Parmesan cheese
salt and black pepper

- Cook the linguine in a large saucepan of lightly salted boiling water for 8–10 minutes or until just tender. Drain well, then return to the pan.

- Meanwhile, heat the oil in a skillet, add the chicken, mushrooms, and pancetta, and cook over high heat for 5–7 minutes, until golden and cooked through.

- Mix together the egg yolks, cream, and Parmesan in a bowl until smooth and season well.

- Add the cooked chicken mixture to the drained linguine, then gently pour the cream mixture over the pasta and, using 2 wooden spoons, toss over low heat until hot and thickened, being careful not to overcook.

 Creamy Chicken, Pancetta, and Mushroom Pasta Cook 10 oz fresh linguine in a saucepan of lightly salted boiling water for 3 minutes or until just tender, then drain. Meanwhile, heat 3 tablespoons olive oil in a skillet, add 4 oz finely chopped pancetta, 2½ cups sliced mushrooms, and 5 oz store-bought cooked chicken breast, thinly sliced, and cook over high heat for 3–4 minutes. Add the drained pasta with ⅔ cup heavy cream and ¼ cup grated Parmesan cheese and toss for 1 minute to coat, then serve.

 Chicken, Pancetta, and Mushroom Pasta Casserole Cook 8 oz penne in a large saucepan of lightly salted boiling water for 8–10 minutes, or according to the package directions, until just tender, then drain and return to the pan. Meanwhile, heat ¼ cup olive oil in a skillet, add 10 oz skinless chicken breasts, cubed, 2 cups thinly sliced cremini mushrooms, and 4 oz coarsely chopped pancetta, and cook over high heat for 5–7 minutes, until browned and cooked through. Add to the drained pasta and toss well. Add 1¼ cups heavy cream and ½ cup grated Parmesan cheese and toss well to coat. Season well, then transfer to a medium gratin dish. Slice a small garlic baguette, then place the slices over the pasta. Sprinkle with 1 cup shredded cheddar cheese. Bake in a preheated oven, at 400°F, for 10 minutes, then transfer to a preheated hot broiler and cook for 2–3 minutes, until piping hot and golden. Serve with a simple salad.

Warm Mediterranean Chicken and Bulgur Wheat Salad

Serves 4

⅓ cup plus 1 tablespoon olive oil

1 large zucchini, cut into thick slices

1 large red onion, cut into thin wedges

1 red bell pepper, cored, seeded, and cut into chunks

½ small eggplant, cut into small chunks

1 garlic clove, thinly sliced

1 cup bulgur wheat

4 boneless, skinless chicken breasts, about 7 oz each

¼ cup chopped parsley

salt and black pepper

- Heat ⅓ cup of the oil in a large skillet, add the zucchini, onion, red bell pepper, eggplant, and garlic, and cook over high heat for 15–20 minutes, stirring almost continuously, until browned and softened.

- Meanwhile, cook the bulgur wheat in a saucepan of lightly salted boiling water for 15 minutes, until tender.

- While the bulgur wheat is cooking, brush the remaining oil over the chicken breasts and season well. Heat a large ridged grill pan until smoking, add the chicken, and cook over high heat for 4–5 minutes on each side, or until browned and cooked through. Remove from the heat and thinly slice diagonally.

- Drain the bulgur wheat. Put into a large bowl, toss with the parsley, and season. Add the hot vegetables and chicken, toss together, and serve.

Mediterranean Chicken Pita

Breads Mix together 1¼ lb thinly sliced skinless chicken breasts and 2 tablespoons olive oil in a large bowl and season well. Heat a large, ridged grill pan until hot, add the chicken, and 2 thinly sliced zucchini, and cook over high heat for 5 minutes, or until cooked through. Add 2 chopped tomatoes and cook for another 2 minutes. Serve in 4 warm pita breads with a handful of arugula leaves in each and spoonfuls of plain yogurt, if desired.

Mediterranean Chicken Kebabs with Herbed Bulgur Wheat

Cook 1½ cups bulgur wheat in a large saucepan of lightly salted boiling water for 15 minutes. Meanwhile, thread 10 oz cubed, skinless chicken breasts, 1 cored, seeded, and cubed red bell pepper, 2 thickly sliced small zucchini, and 2 red onions, cut into wedges, onto 8 metal skewers. Lightly brush with olive oil and season well. Cook under a preheated medium broiler for 8–10 minutes, until browned and cooked through. Drain the bulgur

wheat and put into a large bowl with ½ cup chopped parsley or chives, or both, and toss to mix. Season well, then serve topped with the kebabs.

20 Chicken, Potato, and Spinach Pan-Fry

Serves 2

⅓ cup olive oil

4 white round or red-skinned potatoes, peeled and cubed

8 oz boneless, skinless chicken thighs, cut into thin strips

1 garlic clove, thinly sliced

3 oz prosciutto, torn into pieces

2 tablespoons chopped sage leaves, plus extra leaves to garnish (optional)

1 (5 oz) package baby spinach leaves

1 cup crème fraîche or Greek yogurt

1 tablespoon whole-grain mustard

- Heat the oil in a large skillet, add the potatoes, and cook over high heat for 5 minutes, until starting to turn brown in places.

- Add the chicken and garlic and cook for 5 minutes, until cooked through, then add the prosciutto and sage and cook for another 2 minutes, until the prosciutto is browned and the potatoes are tender. Add the spinach and sauté, stirring, for 1 minute, until wilted.

- Mix together the crème fraîche or Greek yogurt and mustard in a bowl, then spoon into the skillet and cook for 2 minutes, until piping hot. Serve sprinkled with extra sage leaves, if desired.

---

10 Simple Chicken and Spinach with Mashed Potatoes

Heat 2 tablespoons olive oil in a skillet, add 8 oz diced boneless, skinless chicken thighs and 1 sliced garlic clove, and cook for 4–5 minutes, until cooked through. Add 3 oz torn prosciutto and cook for another 2 minutes, then add 1 tablespoon chopped sage leaves and 1 (5 oz) package baby spinach leaves and cook for 2 minutes. Add 1 cup crème fraîche or Greek yogurt and stir for 1 minute, until hot. Serve with cooked mashed potatoes.

30 Chicken, Spinach, and Potato Gratin

Cook 4 peeled and cubed white round or red-skinned potatoes in a saucepan of lightly salted boiling water for 8 minutes, until tender. Meanwhile, heat 3 tablespoons olive oil in a large skillet, add 8 oz boneless, skinless chicken thighs, cut into thin strips, and 1 thinly sliced garlic clove, and cook for 5 minutes, until golden. Add 3 oz prosciutto, torn into pieces, and 2 tablespoons chopped sage leaves and cook for another 3 minutes, until browned and the chicken is cooked through. Drain the potatoes and add to the chicken with 1 (5 oz) package baby spinach leaves and cook for 2 minutes, until wilted. Stir in 1 cup crème fraîche or Greek yogurt and 1 tablespoon whole-grain mustard and toss well. Transfer to a shallow gratin dish and sprinkle with 1 cup shredded cheddar cheese. Cook under a preheated hot broiler for 5 minutes, until golden and bubbling. Serve with salad, if desired.

Roasted Chicken and Spiced Butternut Squash

Serves 2

4 chicken quarters
1 (12 oz) package prepared
  butternut squash pieces
2 tablespoons olive oil
½ red chile, seeded and
  coarsely chopped
1 teaspoon cumin seeds
1 teaspoon ground coriander
½ teaspoon ground paprika
2 tablespoons chopped
  sage leaves
salt and black pepper
sugar snap peas, to serve
  (optional)

- Place the chicken in a roasting pan and season well. Mix together the remaining ingredients in a bowl, making sure the oil and spices thoroughly coat the squash pieces, then arrange around the chicken.

- Place in a preheated oven, at 425°F, for 25 minutes or until the chicken is cooked through and the squash is soft and lightly charred in places. Serve with blanched sugar snap peas, if desired.

---

1 **Spicy Chicken Strips with Sweet Potatoes** Pierce 2 small sweet potatoes several times with a knife. Cook in a microwave on High for 8 minutes or until cooked through. Meanwhile, heat 2 tablespoons olive oil in a skillet, add 10 oz thinly sliced skinless chicken breasts, and cook over high heat for 7–8 minutes, until browned and cooked through. Add ½ teaspoon chili powder, ½ teaspoon ground coriander, and ½ teaspoon cumin seeds and toss again for 1 minute. Cut open each sweet potato and add a pat of butter to each. Serve with the chicken and a handful of arugula leaves.

2 **Spiced Chicken and Butternut Soup** Heat 1 tablespoon olive oil in a large saucepan, add 1 (12 oz) package prepared butternut squash pieces, chopped into smaller pieces, ½ red chile, seeded and coarsely chopped, and 5 oz coarsely chopped skinless chicken breast, and cook for 5 minutes, stirring occasionally. Add 1 teaspoon cumin seeds, 1 teaspoon ground coriander, and 2½ cups hot chicken stock and bring to a boil. Reduce the heat, cover, and simmer for 12 minutes, until the squash is tender and the chicken cooked through. Transfer the mixture to a food processor and process until smooth. Sprinkle with chopped sage leaves, if desired, and serve with warm crusty wheat bread.

 # Asian Chicken Satay Stir-Fry

Serves 2

2 tablespoons sesame oil

10 oz skinless chicken breasts,
cut into long, thick strips

1 bunch of large scallions,
cut in half lengthwise

1 orange bell pepper, cored,
seeded, and cut into thick strips

1 head of bok choy, about 6 oz,
leaves separated

boiled rice, to serve (optional)

For the satay sauce

⅔ cup boiling water

¼ cup smooth peanut butter

2 tablespoons soy sauce

1 tablespoon sweet chili sauce

- Heat the oil in a large wok or skillet, add the chicken strips, and stir-fry over high heat for 5 minutes, until browned in places. Add the scallions and stir-fry for another 3 minutes.

- Add the orange bell pepper and continue to stir-fry for 3 minutes, until the chicken and vegetables are cooked through. Add the bok choy and cook for 1 minute. Remove from the heat.

- To make the sauce, put the measured water into a small saucepan with the remaining ingredients and bring to a boil, stirring with a wire whisk until smooth. Pour into the wok with the chicken and vegetables and toss to coat. Serve immediately with rice, if desired.

 ### Quick Chicken Satay Stir-Fry

Heat 1 tablespoon sesame oil in a wok, add 8 oz chicken strips, and stir-fry over high heat for 5 minutes, until browned. Add 1 (12 oz) package prepared stir-fry vegetables and 4 scallions, coarsely chopped, and stir-fry for another 2–3 minutes, until tender. In a small bowl, mix together 1 tablespoon soy sauce, 2 tablespoons smooth peanut butter, and ¼ cup boiling water. Pour into the wok and toss and cook for another 1 minute. Serve hot.

Satay Chicken Skewers with Asian Vegetable Stir-Fry

Put 2 heaping tablespoons smooth peanut butter, 1 tablespoon soy sauce, 1 tablespoon sweet chili sauce, and ⅓ cup water into a small saucepan and heat gently for about 2 minutes, stirring continuously, until smooth, thick, and warm. Put 10 oz skinless chicken breasts, cut into strips, 1 tablespoon sesame oil, 2 tablespoons soy sauce, and 1 (½ inch) piece of fresh ginger root, peeled and grated, in a bowl and mix well. Let marinate for 5 minutes. Thread the chicken onto 4 presoaked wooden skewers and put on an aluminum foil-lined broiler rack. Cook under a preheated hot broiler for 7–8 minutes, until cooked through, turning halfway through cooking. Meanwhile, heat 1 tablespoon sesame oil in a wok or skillet, add 1 shredded head bok choy, 1 cored, seeded, and thinly sliced orange bell pepper, and 6 coarsely chopped scallions and stir-fry for 3–4 minutes, until softened but still retaining their shape. Serve with the skewers and satay sauce.

10 Spicy Chicken and Plantain with Caribbean Sauce

Serves 2

1 tablespoon sunflower oil

1 small plantain, about 12 oz, peeled and thinly sliced

8 oz skinless chicken breasts, thinly sliced

2 tomatoes, coarsely chopped

⅔ cup coconut milk

⅔ cup tomato puree or tomato sauce

2 tablespoons Jamaican jerk seasoning

1 tablespoon thyme leaves, to garnish (optional)

- Heat the oil in a skillet, add the plantain, and cook over high heat for 2 minutes, stirring occasionally, then remove from the skillet with a slotted spoon and set aside. Add the chicken to the skillet and cook for another 5 minutes, stirring occasionally, until the chicken is golden and cooked through. Return the plantain to the skillet.

- Add the tomatoes, coconut milk, tomato puree or tomato sauce, and jerk seasoning and bring to a boil, then cook for 2 minutes, until piping hot. Spoon into 2 warm serving bowls and sprinkle with the thyme leaves, if using. Serve with rice.

 Spicy Chicken with Plantain Chips

Heat 2 tablespoons oil in a skillet, add 10 oz sliced skinless chicken breasts and 1 chopped onion, and cook over high heat for 5 minutes. Add 1 teaspoon each of ground cumin, ground ginger, ground paprika, and store-bought minced garlic and 1 (14½ oz) can diced tomatoes and bring to a boil. Reduce the heat, cover, and simmer for 10 minutes. Meanwhile, heat ⅔ cup sunflower oil in a deep saucepan until a cube of bread browns in 30 seconds. Cut ½ peeled plantain into slices and deep-fry for about 1 minute, until crisp and golden. Remove with a slotted spoon and drain on paper towels. Season and serve with the chicken.

 Spiced Chicken and Plantain Stew

Heat 2 tablespoons olive oil in a large skillet, add 4 small chicken thighs, and cook over medium heat for 5 minutes, turning once. Add 1 coarsely chopped onion and cook for another 3 minutes, then add 1 crushed garlic clove, 1 cored, seeded, and coarsely chopped red bell pepper, 8 oz peeled and sliced plantain, and 10 okra pods, trimmed and cut in half, and cook for another 3–4 minutes, until the vegetables are starting to soften and the chicken turns brown. Add ½ teaspoon each of ground cloves, ground cinnamon, and ground nutmeg and 1 teaspoon dried thyme and stir to coat. Pour in 1 (14½ oz) can diced tomatoes and ⅔ cup hot chicken stock and bring to a boil, then reduce the heat, cover, and simmer for 15–18 minutes, turning the chicken once, until it is cooked through and the sauce slightly reduced. Serve with rice mixed with kidney beans.

30 Chicken Jalfrezi

Serves 2

2 tablespoons sunflower oil
10 oz skinless chicken breasts,
  cut into pieces
1 onion, cut into slim wedges
1 small green bell pepper, cored,
  seeded, and cut into chunks
1 green chile, seeded and finely
  chopped
1 teaspoon ground cumin
1 teaspoon garam masala
½ teaspoon turmeric
2 tomatoes, cut into wedges
2 tablespoons plain yogurt
1 cup water
warm naan, to serve

- Heat the oil in a large skillet, add the chicken, onion, and green bell pepper, and cook over medium heat for 10 minutes, until starting to turn brown. Add the chile and spices and cook for 2–3 minutes, then add the tomatoes and cook for another 3 minutes.

- Stir in the yogurt, then pour in the measured water, cover, and simmer gently for 10 minutes, until the chicken is cooked through and the flavors have developed, stirring occasionally and adding a little more water, if necessary. Serve with warm naan to mop up the juices.

---

10 Speedy Chicken Curry

Heat 2 tablespoons sunflower oil in a skillet over high heat, add 10 oz thinly sliced skinless chicken breasts, and cook for 5 minutes, until browned and cooked through. Add ½ seeded and coarsely chopped red chile and cook for another 1 minute, then add 1¼ cups of jalfrezi sauce from a jar and heat through for 2–3 minutes. Stir in ¼ cup plain yogurt and serve with cooked pilaf rice or other long-grain rice, if desired.

20 Spicy Chicken Stir-Fry

Heat 1 tablespoon sunflower oil in a wok, add 10 oz coarsely chopped skinless chicken breasts and 1 large onion, cut into thin wedges, and stir-fry over medium-high heat for 5–6 minutes, until the chicken is browned and cooked through and the onion is softened. Add ½ seeded and coarsely chopped green chile and cook for another 1 minute, then add 1 (12 oz) package prepared stir-fry vegetables and 2 teaspoons garam masala and stir-fry for 3–4 minutes, until the vegetables are softened. Spoon into chapattis, roll up, and serve.

MID-CHIC-LOI

3⃝ Honeyed Chicken and Roasted Rosemary Vegetables

Serves 4

8 chicken thighs, about
 3½–4 oz each
6 small parsnips, peeled and
 halved lengthwise
8 small carrots, trimmed and
 halved lengthwise
2 small turnips, peeled and cut
 into thin wedges
⅓ cup olive oil
2 tablespoons rosemary leaves
¼ cup honey
salt and black pepper
2 small handfuls of thyme,
 to garnish

- Put the chicken into a large roasting pan and season well. Place the vegetables around the chicken, drizzle with the oil, and toss. Sprinkle with the rosemary and season.

- Roast in a preheated oven, at 425°F, for 25 minutes or until browned and cooked through. Drizzle with the honey and, using 2 spoons, toss well. Return to the oven and cook for another 2 minutes. Serve sprinkled with the thyme.

1⃝ Simple Honeyed Rosemary Chicken and Vegetables Heat ¼ cup olive oil in a large skillet, add 1 lb thinly sliced skinless chicken breasts and 6 peeled and thinly sliced carrots, and cook over medium heat for 5–7 minutes, until browned and cooked through. Add 2 tablespoons coarsely chopped rosemary leaves and ⅔ cup white wine, stir, and let boil until almost all the wine evaporates, then add ¼ cup honey and toss well for 1 minute. Season well, then serve with cooked rice, if desired.

2⃝ Rosemary and Honey-Glazed Chicken and Vegetables Heat ¼ cup olive oil in a large skillet, add 4 parsnips, peeled and coarsely chopped, 2 onions, cut into thin wedges, and 8 carrots, peeled and coarsely chopped, and cook over medium heat for 5 minutes, until just tender. Add 1 lb skinless chicken breasts, cut into chunks, and cook, turning and stirring, for another 8–10 minutes, until cooked through, reducing the heat if the vegetables become too browned. Add

2 tablespoons chopped rosemary leaves and ¼ cup honey and toss and stir for 1 minute. Serve hot.

10 Creamy Chicken, Ham, and Leek Pan-Fry

Serves 2

1 tablespoon olive oil

1 tablespoon butter

8 oz skinless chicken breasts, cut into chunks

4 oz cured ham, cubed

1 leek, trimmed, cleaned and thinly sliced

1 cup crème fraîche or Greek yogurt

1 tablespoon whole-grain mustard

1 teaspoon Dijon mustard

cooked rice, mashed potatoes, or warm crusty bread, to serve

- Heat the oil and butter in a skillet, add the chicken and ham, and cook over high heat for 5 minutes. Add the leek and cook for another 3 minutes, stirring almost continuously, until the leek is slightly golden and softened and the chicken is cooked through.

- Mix together the crème fraîche or Greek yogurt and mustards in a bowl, then stir into the chicken and ham and heat through for 1 minute, until piping hot. Serve with rice, mashed potatoes, or warm crusty bread.

20 Leek-Stuffed Chicken in Prosciutto

Heat 1 tablespoon olive oil in a skillet, add 1 small trimmed, cleaned, and thinly sliced leek, and cook for 3–4 minutes, until softened. Make a slit lengthwise in 2 boneless, skinless chicken breasts, about 5 oz each, to form pockets. Place 1 slice of Gruyère, about 1 oz, into each pocket, then fill with the leek mixture. Tightly wrap each with 1 slice of prosciutto to secure the filling. Heat 1 tablespoon olive oil in the skillet and cook the chicken over medium heat for 10–12 minutes, turning frequently, until browned and cooked through.

30 Creamy Chicken, Ham, and Leek Gratin

Heat 2 tablespoons olive oil in a skillet, add 10 oz skinless chicken breasts, cut into chunks, and 4 oz cubed cured ham, and cook for 5 minutes, until starting to turn brown. Add 1 large trimmed, cleaned, and sliced leek, and cook for another 3 minutes, until the chicken is cooked through, then set aside. In a separate saucepan, melt 2 tablespoons butter, add 3 tablespoons all-purpose flour, and cook for a few seconds, stirring. Remove from the heat and gradually add 1¼ cups milk. Return to the heat and bring to a boil, stirring continuously, until boiled and thickened. Stir in 1 tablespoon Dijon mustard and 1 tablespoon whole-grain mustard. Stir the chicken and leek mixture into the sauce, then transfer to a shallow ovenproof dish and sprinkle with ¼ cup fresh whole-wheat bread crumbs and 2 tablespoons grated Parmesan cheese. Cook under a preheated hot broiler for 2–3 minutes, until golden and bubbling.

QuickCook
Fish and Seafood

Recipes listed by cooking time

3⟨clock⟩

2⟨clock⟩

20 Mussels with Cider and Garlic Sauce

Serves 2

2 lb fresh mussels
1 tablespoon butter
1 garlic clove, chopped
½ cup hard dry cider
2 tablespoons heavy cream
1 tablespoon chopped thyme
  leaves
salt and black pepper
crusty bread, to serve

- Wash the mussels under cold running water and discard any that are open or don't shut when tapped. Pull off any fibrous "beards" and remove any barnacles, then rinse again.

- Heat the butter in a large saucepan, add the garlic, and cook gently for 1 minute. Add the mussels and then the cider. Bring to a boil, cover, and cook for 3–4 minutes, shaking the pan occasionally until the mussels have opened.

- Using a slotted spoon, transfer the mussels to 2 warm serving bowls, discarding any that remain closed. Reheat the pan juices, add the cream and thyme, and season. Pour the sauce over the mussels and serve with plenty of crusty bread.

 Mussel, Garlic, and Cider Tagliatelle

Put 1¼ lb cooked mussels in garlic butter in a large saucepan, add ½ cup hard dry cider and 2 tablespoons crème fraîche or heavy cream, and heat through for 5 minutes, until piping hot. Meanwhile, cook 10 oz fresh egg tagliatelle in a saucepan of lightly salted boiling water for 3 minutes or according to the package directions, until just tender. Drain, then add to the mussel pan and stir to coat in the sauce. Serve sprinkled with chopped parsley.

 Garlicky Cider Mussels with Fries

Cut 2 scrubbed baking potatoes into fries, put on a baking sheet, and drizzle with 1 tablespoon olive oil. Season and bake in a preheated oven, at 400°F, for 25 minutes, turning occasionally, until golden and cooked. Meanwhile, wash 2 lb fresh mussels under cold running water and discard any that don't shut when tapped. Pull off any fibrous "beards" and remove any barnacles, then rinse again. Heat 1 tablespoon butter in a large saucepan, add 2 chopped garlic cloves and 2 chopped shallots, and cook for 1 minute, then tip in the mussels and add ½ cup hard dry cider. Bring to a boil, cover, and cook for 3–4 minutes, shaking the pan occasionally until the mussels have opened. Using a slotted spoon, transfer the mussels to 2 warm serving bowls, discarding any that remain closed. Reheat the pan juices and stir in 2 tablespoons crème fraîche or heavy cream and 1 tablespoon chopped parsley. Season and pour the sauce over the mussels. Serve with the fries.

Crispy Pesto Baked Cod

Serves 2

2 pieces of skinless cod fillet,
about 6 oz each
4 teaspoons pesto
½ cup fresh white bread crumbs
¼ cup grated Parmesan cheese
8 cherry tomatoes, halved
8 ripe black olives, pitted
2 tablespoons olive oil
salt and black pepper

To serve

new potatoes
peas

- Place the fish on a baking sheet and spread the pesto over the top. Mix together the bread crumbs and Parmesan in a bowl, then season. Spoon the bread crumb mixture over the pesto.

- Add the tomatoes and olives to the baking sheet and drizzle with the oil. Bake in a preheated oven, at 425°F, for 15 minutes or until the fish is cooked through. Serve with new potatoes and peas.

 Fish Stick Baguettes with Pesto Mayo Cook 6 fish sticks under a preheated medium broiler for 8 minutes, turning once, until golden and cooked through. Meanwhile, cut 2 (6 inch) pieces of French bread in half and toast the cut sides. Mix 2 teaspoons pesto with 2 tablespoons mayonnaise in a small bowl, then spread over the toasted bread. Top with salad greens and the fish sticks.

 Pesto Fish Casserole Heat 1 tablespoon olive oil in a skillet, add 10 oz skinless cod fillet, and sauté for 8–10 minutes, turning occasionally, until cooked through. Remove from the skillet. Add 1 tablespoon pesto and ¼ cup crème fraîche or heavy cream to the skillet and heat through, stirring, then break the fish into chunks, add to the sauce, and simmer for a few minutes. Meanwhile, heat 2 cups cooked mashed potatoes for a few minutes until heated through. Spoon the fish and sauce into a flameproof dish and spoon the mashed potatoes over the top. Sprinkle with ¼ cup shredded cheddar cheese, then cook under a preheated medium broiler for 5 minutes, until crisp and golden. Serve with peas.

Tuna and Bean Pasta Salad

Serves 2

5 oz penne

¾ cup trimmed and halved green beans

1 (5 oz) can chunk light tuna in oil, drained and broken into chunks

¾ cup canned rinsed and drained kidney beans

¼ cup drained and chopped roasted red peppers from a jar

2 scallions, chopped

1 tablespoon balsamic vinegar

½ teaspoon Dijon mustard

3 tablespoons olive oil

salt and black pepper

- Cook the penne in a saucepan of lightly salted boiling water for 10 minutes, or according to the package directions, until just tender, adding the green beans for the final 5 minutes. Drain and rinse under cold running water, then drain again.

- Place the pasta and green beans in a bowl with the tuna, kidney beans, roasted peppers, and scallions.

- In a small bowl, whisk together the vinegar, mustard, and oil. Season, then pour the dressing over the salad and toss lightly to mix.

 Tuna and Bean Pita Pockets

Drain 1 (5 oz) can tuna in oil and break into chunks. Place in a bowl and add ¾ cup rinsed and drained, canned mixed beans, 2 chopped scallions, and 8 pitted and chopped ripe black olives. Spoon over 3 tablespoons prepared French dressing and mix well. Warm 2 pita breads, cut in half, and open out into pockets. Fill with the tuna and bean mixture and some butterhead lettuce.

 Niçoise Pasta Salad

Cook 5 oz penne or other pasta in a saucepan of lightly salted boiling water for 10 minutes, or according to the package directions, until just tender, adding ¾ cup trimmed green beans for the final 5 minutes. Drain and rinse under cold running water, then drain again. In a separate small saucepan, boil 2 eggs for 8 minutes, then drain and let cool in cold water. Arrange the pasta and beans on a serving plate. Add 1 (5 oz) can chunk light tuna in oil, drained and broken into chunks, 2 tomatoes, cut into wedges, and 8 ripe black olives. Shell the eggs, cut in half, and place on the salad. Mix together 1 tablespoon balsamic vinegar, ½ teaspoon Dijon mustard, and 3 tablespoons olive oil in a bowl. Season and drizzle the dressing over the salad.

Spicy Squid with Fries and Garlic Mayo

Serves 4

4 baking potatoes, about 6 oz each, scrubbed
¼ cup olive oil
2 garlic cloves, crushed
½ cup mayonnaise
vegetable or peanut oil, for deep-frying
1½ lb prepared squid, sliced
salt and black pepper
lemon wedges, to serve

For the batter

1¼ cups all-purpose flour
2 tablespoons cornstarch
2 teaspoons coarsely ground black pepper
1 teaspoon dried red pepper flakes
1 teaspoon sea salt flakes
1¾ cups chilled sparkling water

- Cut the potatoes into fries, toss with the olive oil, and season. Spread out over a large baking sheet and bake in a preheated oven, at 400°F, for 25 minutes, turning occasionally, until golden and tender.

- Meanwhile, mix together the garlic and mayonnaise in a serving bowl and set aside. Fill a deep saucepan halfway with vegetable or peanut oil and heat to 375°F, or until a cube of bread browns in 30 seconds.

- Make the batter. Place the flour and cornstarch in a bowl, add the black pepper, red pepper flakes, and salt flakes and quickly stir in the sparkling water to make a light batter. Do not overmix; it doesn't matter if it's still a little lumpy.

- Quickly dip the squid pieces in the batter and drain off the excess. Deep-fry in batches in the hot oil for 2–3 minutes, until crisp and golden. Remove with a slotted spoon and drain on paper towels. Serve with the fries, garlic mayonnaise, and lemon wedges.

---

1 Crispy Squid with Chili Dipping Sauce

Dust 12 oz prepared squid rings in seasoned flour, then pan-fry, in batches if necessary, in hot vegetable or peanut oil for 2–3 minutes, until crisp and golden. Remove with a slotted spoon and drain on paper towels. Serve as an appetizer with a sweet chili dipping sauce, lime wedges, and crusty bread.

2 Spicy Cornmeal Squid with Lime Mayo

Fill a deep saucepan halfway with vegetable or peanut oil and heat to 375°F, or until a cube of bread browns in 30 seconds. Meanwhile, put ½ cup cornmeal, 1 teaspoon coarsely crushed black peppercorns, 1 teaspoon dried red pepper flakes, and 2 pinches of sea salt flakes in a large freezer bag. Add 1½ lb prepared squid rings to the bag and shake to coat in the mixture. Deep-fry in batches in the hot oil for 2–3 minutes, until crisp and golden. Remove with a slotted spoon and drain on paper towels. Serve with oven fries and mayonnaise mixed with a little lime rind.

30 Ginger and Lime Mackerel with Roasted Vegetables

Serves 2

1 small fennel bulb, trimmed
    and sliced

8 new potatoes, thickly sliced

2 tomatoes, cut into wedges

2 tablespoons olive oil

½ teaspoon fennel seeds

2 whole mackerel

1 tablespoon soy sauce

½ inch piece of fresh ginger root,
    peeled and grated

finely grated rind and juice of
    1 lime

1 teaspoon honey

salt and black pepper

lime wedges, to serve

- Spread the fennel, potatoes, and tomatoes over a baking pan, drizzle with the oil, sprinkle with the fennel seeds, and season. Place in a preheated oven, at 400°F, for 25 minutes, turning occasionally, until cooked and lightly charred.

- Meanwhile, slash the mackerel skin several times and season both sides, then place on an aluminum foil-lined broiler rack, skin side up. Mix together the soy sauce, ginger, lime rind and juice and honey in a small bowl and drizzle half of it over the fish.

- Cook under a preheated hot broiler until the skin starts to crisp. Turn the fish over, drizzle with the remaining soy mixture, and broil for another 2–3 minutes, until the mackerel is cooked through and flakes easily. Serve with the roasted vegetables and lime wedges.

---

10 Pan-Fried Ginger and Lime Mackerel with Roasted Vegetable Couscous Put ½ cup roasted vegetable-flavored couscous in a heatproof bowl and just cover with boiling water. Cover with plastic wrap and let stand for 5–8 minutes, or according to the package directions. Meanwhile, heat 1 tablespoon olive oil in a skillet. Lightly dust 2 mackerel fillets in flour, then add to the skillet, skin side down, and cook for 2 minutes, until the skin is crisp. Turn the fish over and cook for another 2–3 minutes, until the mackerel is cooked through. Add ¼ cup store-bought chili, cilantro, and ginger salad dressing and the juice of ½ lime to the skillet, heat through, and spoon the sauce over the fish to coat. Fluff up the couscous with a fork and serve with the mackerel fillets, pan juices, and lime wedges.

20 Ginger and Lime Mackerel with Fennel Salad and New Potatoes Cook 8 oz new potatoes in a saucepan of lightly salted boiling water for 15 minutes, until tender. Thinly slice ½ trimmed fennel bulb and 4 radishes. Mix together in a bowl and drizzle with a little white wine vinegar and olive oil. Set aside. Meanwhile, prepare and broil the Ginger and Lime Mackerel as above. Drain the potatoes and lightly crush with a potato masher, then drizzle with a little olive oil and season. Serve the mackerel with the potatoes and fennel salad.

Baked Anchovy Tomatoes with Spaghetti

Serves 4

8 ripe tomatoes, quartered
8 anchovy fillets in oil, drained and chopped
2 garlic cloves, crushed
1⅔ cups crumbled feta cheese
2 small handfuls of basil leaves, plus extra to garnish
¼ cup olive oil
4 slices of ciabatta bread, torn into pieces
8 oz spaghetti
salt and black pepper

- Sprinkle the tomatoes, anchovies, garlic, feta, and basil over a large baking sheet. Drizzle with half the oil and season with black pepper (the anchovies are salty, so do not add salt). Bake in a preheated oven, at 375°F, for 20 minutes, turning occasionally, until the tomatoes are soft.

- Sprinkle the bread over a separate baking sheet and drizzle with the remaining oil. Bake in the oven for the final 10 minutes of the baking time for the tomatoes.

- Meanwhile, cook the spaghetti in a large saucepan of lightly salted boiling water for 10 minutes or according to the package directions, until just tender, then drain and return to the pan. Lightly crush the tomato mixture with a fork, add the bread, and toss with the spaghetti. Serve sprinkled with a few extra basil leaves.

 ### Anchovy Tomato Toasts

Heat 2 tablespoons olive oil in a flameproof skillet, add 8 thickly sliced tomatoes, 2 crushed garlic cloves, and 8 drained anchovy fillets in oil, chopped, and sauté for 2–3 minutes, turning occasionally, until the tomatoes are soft. Sprinkle with 2 small handfuls of basil leaves, a drizzle of balsamic vinegar, and 8 oz chopped mozzarella cheese. Season with black pepper and put the skillet under a preheated medium broiler for 2–3 minutes, until the cheese is melted and bubbling. Serve spooned over toasted ciabatta bread.

 ### Spaghetti Puttanesca

Heat ¼ cup olive oil in a large skillet, add 2 crushed garlic cloves and 8–12 coarsely chopped tomatoes, and cook for 2 minutes, stirring. Add 4 drained anchovy fillets in oil, chopped, 1 teaspoon dried red pepper flakes, 4 teaspoons drained capers, and 2 tablespoons tomato paste. Simmer, stirring, for 5 minutes, adding a little water if the sauce is too thick. Season with black pepper. Cook 8 oz spaghetti in a large saucepan of lightly salted boiling water for 10 minutes or according to the package direcions, until just tender. Drain and toss with the sauce, adding 16 pitted ripe black olives.

Smoked Haddock on Toast

Serves 2

2 tablespoons butter

3 tablespoons all-purpose flour

⅔ cup milk

¼ cup beer

½ teaspoon English mustard

1 teaspoon Worcestershire sauce

2 tablespoons grated Parmesan cheese

2 pieces of smoked haddock fillet, about 6 oz each

1 tomato, sliced

4 cups spinach leaves, rinsed

salt and black pepper

- Melt the butter in a saucepan, add the flour, and cook for 1 minute, stirring. Remove from the heat and gradually add the milk and beer. Return to the heat and bring to a boil, stirring continuously until thickened. Add the mustard, Worcestershire sauce, and two-thirds of the cheese. Stir well and season.

- Place the fish in a buttered baking dish, spoon the cheese sauce over the fish, and put the tomato slices on top. Sprinkle with the remaining cheese and bake in a preheated oven, at 400°F, for 12–15 minutes, until golden and the fish is cooked through.

- Toward the end of the cooking time, put the spinach in a saucepan without any extra water. Cover and cook for 2 minutes, until just wilted, then drain. Serve with the fish.

Quick Hot-Smoked Haddock on Toast

Heat ¾ cup store-bought fresh cheese sauce, a dash of Worcestershire sauce, and 2 tablespoons beer in a small saucepan. Stir in 7 oz hot-smoked haddock or 4 oz smoked mackerel, skinned and flaked, and heat through. Toast 4 thick slices of wheat bread on both sides, put on an aluminum foil-lined broiler rack, and spoon the fish mixture and ½ cup shredded cheddar cheese oer the toast. Add 4 tomato halves to the broiler rack. Cook under a preheated medium broiler for 2–3 minutes, until bubbling.

Smoked Haddock Tart

Put 8 oz smoked haddock fillet in a shallow saucepan. Pour ⅔ cup milk over the fish and bring to a boil, then reduce the heat and simmer for 3–4 minutes, until cooked through. Remove the fish from the pan and reserve the milk. Melt 2 tablespoons butter in a saucepan, add 3 tablespoons all-purpose flour, and cook for 1 minute. Remove from the heat and gradually add the reserved milk and ¼ cup beer. Return to the heat and bring to a boil, stirring until thickened. Stir in ½ teaspoon English mustard, 1 teaspoon Worcestershire sauce, and ½ cup shredded cheddar cheese and season. Flake the fish, discarding the skin, and stir into the sauce. Place ½ sheet of ready-to-bake puff pastry on a baking sheet. Spread the fish mixture over the pastry, leaving a ½ inch border around the edge. Top with 1 sliced tomato and sprinkle with ½ cup shredded cheddar cheese. Bake in a preheated oven, at 400°F, for 15 minutes, until golden and the pastry is crisp. Serve warm with salad.

20 Teriyaki Salmon with Egg Noodles

Serves 2

1 garlic clove, crushed

2 teaspoons sesame oil

3 tablespoons teriyaki sauce

2 pieces of salmon fillet, about
5 oz each, with skin on

1 tablespoon vegetable oil

5 oz medium egg noodles

½ cup frozen edamame
(soybeans) or peas

1 tablespoon sweet sherry

1 tablespoon soy sauce

1 teaspoon toasted sesame seeds

To garnish

2 scallions, cut into thin strips

1 tablespoon chopped cilantro
leaves

- Mix together the garlic, 1 teaspoon of the sesame oil, and the teriyaki sauce in a shallow dish. Add the salmon and turn to coat in the sauce.

- Heat the vegetable oil in a skillet, add the salmon, and cook, skin side down, for 3–4 minutes, until crisp, then turn the fish over and cook for another 8–10 minutes, until cooked through.

- Meanwhile, cook the noodles and edamame or peas in a saucepan of lightly salted boiling water for 3 minutes, until tender. Drain and return to the pan. Add the remaining sesame oil, the sherry, and soy sauce and toss to coat.

- Pour any remaining teriyaki marinade into the salmon pan and heat through. Sprinkle with the sesame seeds and serve with the noodles, topped with the scallions and cilantro.

 **Teriyaki Salmon
Stir-Fry**

Toss 10 oz skinless salmon fillet, cut into chunks, in 2 tablespoons teriyaki sauce. Heat 1 tablespoon vegetable oil in a wok, add the salmon, and cook, gently stirring occasionally, for about 5 minutes or until cooked through. Add 1 tablespoon soy sauce and a squeeze of lime juice. Meanwhile, soak 5 oz cellophane rice noodles in boiling water for 3 minutes. Drain and return to the pan. Add 2 thinly sliced scallions and 1 tablespoon chopped cilantro and toss to mix. Serve the fish with the noodles.

 **Teriyaki Salmon
with Sesame**

Broccoli Mix together 1 crushed garlic clove, 1 teaspoon sesame oil, and 3 tablespoons teriyaki sauce in a shallow dish. Add 2 pieces of salmon fillet, about 5 oz each, turn to coat in the sauce, and let marinate for 10 minutes. Heat 1 tablespoon vegetable oil in a skillet, add the salmon, and sauté for 10–15 minutes, turning occasionally, until cooked through. Pour in any remaining teriyaki sauce and heat through. Meanwhile, heat 1 teaspoon sesame oil and 1 tablespoon

vegetable oil in a wok or skillet, add 1 crushed garlic clove and 1 teaspoon peeled and grated fresh ginger root, and cook for 1 minute. Add 8 oz baby broccoli and stir-fry for 2 minutes. Pour in a little boiling water, cover, and steam for 5 minutes, until just tender. Add 1 tablespoon soy sauce and a squeeze of lime juice, then sprinkle with sesame seeds. Serve the salmon and broccoli with rice or noodles.

3 Thai Crab Cakes with Carrot Noodle Salad

Serves 2

½ red chile, seeded
2 scallions
1 tablespoon cilantro leaves
1 tablespoon Thai red curry paste
1 teaspoon Thai fish sauce
7 oz skinless white fish fillets
1 (6 oz) can crabmeat, drained
1 medium egg
5 oz cellophane rice noodles
1 cup halved sugar snap peas
   (halved lengthwise)
1 carrot, shredded
2 tablespoons vegetable oil
lime wedges, to serve

For the dipping sauce

3 tablespoons light soy sauce
juice of ½ lime
1 teaspoon Thai fish sauce
pinch of sugar
½ red chile, thinly sliced

- Place the chile, scallions, and cilantro in a food processor and pulse until chopped. Add the curry paste and fish sauce, then pulse again to mix. Add the fish, crabmeat, and egg and pulse until the mixture is well mixed but not smooth. Using wet hands, shape the mixture into 8 crab cakes. Cover and chill in the refrigerator for 10 minutes.

- Meanwhile, mix together the dipping sauce ingredients and set aside. Soak the noodles in boiling water for a few minutes to soften. Drain and rinse under cold water, then drain again and place in a bowl. Add the sugar snap peas, carrot, and a little of the dipping sauce and mix well.

- Heat the vegetable oil in a skillet, add the crab cakes, and cook for 5 minutes, turning once, until golden and cooked through. Drain on paper towels and serve with the noodle salad, dipping sauce, and lime wedges.

 Thai Crab and Carrot Salad
Soak 5 oz cellophane rice noodles in boiling water for 3 minutes to soften. Drain and rinse in a colander, then place in a bowl. Add 1 (6 oz) can crabmeat, drained, 1 cup sugar snap peas, 1 shredded carrot, and ¼ cup chopped cilantro. Mix together 1 teaspoon Thai red curry paste, 1 teaspoon Thai fish sauce, the juice of ½ lim,e and 1 teaspoon soy sauce. Toss through the salad to mix.

 Quick Thai Crab Cakes with Carrot Salad Put 8 oz skinless white fish fillets, such as cod, red snapper, or Alaskan pollock, 1 (6 oz) can crabmeat, drained, 1 tablespoon Thai red curry paste, 1 tablespoon cilantro leaves, and 1 teaspoon Thai fish sauce in a food processor. Pulse until well mixed but not smooth. Using wet hands, shape the mixture into 8 cakes. Cover and chill for 5 minutes. Mix 2 cups shredded napa cabbage with 1 shredded carrot and 1 sliced scallion. Mix together 2 teaspoons rice wine vinegar, a pinch of sugar, and 2 teaspoons sesame oil. Add to the salad and toss to coat. Heat 1 tablespoon vegetable oil in a skillet, add the crab cakes, and cook for 5 minutes, turning once, until golden and cooked through. Serve with the salad and sweet chili dipping sauce.

30 Seafood Tagliatelle

Serves 4

2 tablespoons olive oil

1 onion, chopped

2 garlic cloves, crushed

1 (14½ oz) can diced tomatoes

½ cup dry white wine

2 pinches of sugar

8 oz tagliatelle

1 (1 lb) package mixed seafood, thawed if frozen

salt and black pepper

2 tablespoons chopped parsley, to garnish

- Heat the oil in a large skillet, add the onion and garlic, and cook over low heat for 3 minutes, until slightly softened. Add the tomatoes, wine, and sugar and season. Bring to a boil, then reduce the heat and simmer gently for 15–20 minutes, stirring occasionally and adding a little water if the sauce is too thick.

- Meanwhile, cook the tagliatelle in a large saucepan of lightly salted boiling water for about 8 minutes, or according to the package directions, until just tender.

- Stir the seafood into the sauce and heat through for a few minutes until piping hot. Drain the tagliatelle, then add to the seafood sauce and toss to coat. Serve sprinkled with the parsley.

 ### Creamy Seafood Pasta

Cook 1 lb fresh egg tagliatelle in a large saucepan of lightly salted boiling water for 3 minutes, or according to the package directions, until just tender. Meanwhile, heat 1 cup heavy cream, ½ cup dry white wine, 2 crushed garlic cloves, and 2 tablespoons chopped dill in a large saucepan. Add 1 (1 lb) package mixed seafood, thawed if frozen, heat through for a few minutes until piping hot, and season. Drain the pasta, add to the sauce, and toss to coat. Serve sprinkled with extra dill.

 ### Simple Seafood Risotto

Cook 2 (8 oz) packages quick-cooking saffron risotto rice according to the package directions, adding 4 tablespoons butter to the pan with the water. Add 1 cup frozen peas for the final 3 minutes. Stir in 1 (1 lb) package mixed seafood, thawed if frozen, 2 tablespoons shredded basil leaves, and ½ cup grated Parmesan cheese and gently heat through for a few minutes until piping hot. Serve with a sprinkling of Parmesan and black pepper.

30 Asparagus, Lemon, and Herb-Stuffed Salmon

Serves 4

20 fine asparagus spears, trimmed
butter, for greasing
8 pieces of salmon fillet, about 4 oz each, skinned
finely grated rind and juice of 1 lemon
¼ cup chopped parsley
2 tablespoons chopped dill
salt and black pepper

To serve

new potatoes
salad (optional)

- Cook the asparagus in a large saucepan of lightly salted boiling water for 3–4 minutes, until just tender. Drain well.

- Lightly grease a baking sheet, then put 4 salmon fillets on the sheet, skinned side up. Toss the asparagus with the lemon rind, parsley, and dill and season well. Arrange on top of the salmon fillets, then top with the remaining salmon fillets, skinned side down. Using 3 pieces of kitchen string on each, roughly tie the salmon pieces together to enclose the filling. Season and pour over the lemon juice.

- Place in a preheated oven, at 425°F, for 10 minutes or until the fish is opaque and cooked through. Serve with new potatoes and salad, if desired.

---

10 Broiled Lemon Salmon with Asparagus Put 4 salmon fillets, about 4 oz each, on an aluminum foil-lined broiler rack and season well with black pepper. Finely grate 2 lemons, sprinkle the rind over the top of each, and press into the fish, then squeeze the juice from the lemons over the fish. Cook under a preheated hot broiler for 4–5 minutes or until opaque and cooked through. Meanwhile, heat ¼ cup olive oil in a large saucepan, add 20 trimmed asparagus spears, and cook over high heat for 5 minutes, stirring and tossing until tender. Serve with the broiled salmon.

20 Lemony Salmon and Asparagus Cook 2 bunches of trimmed and coarsely chopped asparagus spears in a large saucepan of lightly salted boiling water for 2 minutes, then immediately drain and rinse under cold running water. Set aside. Heat ¼ cup olive oil in a large wok or skillet, add 1¼ lb cubed skinless salmon fillet, and cook for 5–6 minutes, turning frequently without breaking up the pieces, until browned all over and cooked through. Put the finely grated rind and juice of 2 lemons in a bowl, stir in 1¾ cups crème fraîche or heavy cream, and season well. Spoon into the pan, add the drained asparagus, and heat through for 2 minutes, until the sauce is piping hot. Serve hot.

30 Shrimp Jambalaya

Serves 4

2 tablespoons olive oil
1 large green bell pepper, cored,
    seeded, and thinly sliced
4 celery sticks, thinly sliced
12 oz cooked, peeled
    jumbo shrimp
2 tablespoons Cajun seasoning
2 (15 oz) cans kidney beans,
    rinsed and drained
4 large fresh tomatoes,
    coarsely chopped
1¼ cups hot fish stock
1 cup shredded fresh coconut
1⅓ cups quick-cooking basmati
    rice or other long-grain rice
salt and black pepper
thyme, to garnish

- Heat the oil in a large skillet, add the green bell pepper and celery, and cook over medium heat for 7–8 minutes, until starting to soften. Add the shrimp and Cajun seasoning and sauté, stirring, for 5 minutes.

- Add the kidney beans, tomatoes, stock, and coconut and bring to a boil, then reduce the heat, cover, and simmer for 10 minutes, stirring occasionally, until piping hot.

- Meanwhile, cook the rice in a large saucepan of lightly salted boiling water for 15–20 minutes, or according to the package directions, until tender. Drain well, then add to the shrimp mixture and cook for another 2 minutes, stirring occasionally, until piping hot. Season well and serve garnished with thyme.

 Cajun-Spiced Shrimp

Heat 2 tablespoons olive oil in a large skillet, add 1 thinly sliced onion, and cook for 3 minutes. Add 1 lb cooked, peeled jumbo shrimp and cook over high heat for 2 minutes, then add 2 teaspoons Cajun seasoning and 4 coarsely chopped tomatoes and cook for another 2–3 minutes, until piping hot. Add ½ cup coconut milk and heat for a few seconds, then stir in ¼ cup chopped cilantro leaves. Serve with cooked rice.

 Cajun Shrimp Rice and Peas

Put 1⅓ cups quick-cooking basmati rice or other long-grain rice, 2½ cups hot chicken stock, and 1¾ cups can coconut milk in a large saucepan and bring to a boil. Reduce the heat, cover, and simmer for 12–15 minutes, until the rice is tender, adding a little more water if necessary. Meanwhile, heat 2 tablespoons olive oil in a large skillet, add 2 onions, cut into thin wedges, and cook for 5 minutes, until golden and softened, then add

12 oz cooked, peeled shrimp and 4 teaspoons Cajun seasoning and cook over high heat for 3–4 minutes, until the shrimp and onions are sizzling. Add 1 (15 oz) can kidney beans, rinsed and drained, to the rice and stir through, then add the shrimp and onions and toss to mix. Serve sprinkled with chopped cilantro leaves.

MID-FISH-FAT

3 Smoked Fish and Fennel Casserole

Serves 2

2 tablespoons butter
1 onion, finely sliced
1 small or ½ fennel bulb,
   trimmed and finely sliced
12 oz skinless smoked haddock
   fillet, cubed
4 oz smoked salmon
1 cup crème fraîche or
   heavy cream
juice of ½ lemon
2 tablespoons water
2 cups cooked mashed potatoes
⅓ cup chopped parsley
2 tablespoons chopped dill
¼ cup grated smoked
   cheddar cheese

- Heat the butter in a saucepan, add the onion and fennel, and cook over medium heat for 5 minutes, until softened. Transfer to a bowl, add the smoked fish, crème fraîche, and lemon juice, and toss together, adding the measured water to loosen.

- Spoon into 2 individual gratin dishes. Place the mashed potatoes in a bowl, add the herbs, and mix well. Spoon the potatoes over the fish, then sprinkle with the cheese. Put into a preheated oven, at 425°F, for 15–20 minutes, until heated through.

- Place the dishes under a preheated hot broiler for 1 minute until golden.

 Smoked Fish and Fennel Pan-Fry

Heat 2 tablespoons butter in a skillet, add 1 small finely sliced onion and ½ trimmed and finely sliced fennel bulb, and cook for 3–4 minutes, until softened. Stir in 1 cup crème fraîche or heavy cream and the juice of ½ lemon and heat for 1 minute. Add 8 oz cubed, skinless smoked haddock fillet, 4 oz smoked salmon, and 1 tablespoon chopped dill. Bring to a boil, then reduce the heat, cover, and simmer for 3–4 minutes, until the fish is cooked through.

 Smoked Fish and Fennel Tortillas

Heat 2 tablespoons butter in a skillet, add 1 small finely sliced onion and ½ small trimmed and finely sliced fennel bulb, and cook for 3–4 minutes, until softened. Remove from the heat and add 12 oz cubed skinless smoked haddock fillet, 4 oz smoked salmon, and ⅓ cup water. Return to the heat and bring to a boil, then reduce the heat, cover, and simmer for 3 minutes, until the fish is opaque and cooked through.

Spoon in 1 cup crème fraîche or heavy cream and the juice of ½ lemon and heat for another 1 minute. Stir in 1 tablespoon chopped dill. Spoon the mixture onto 4 tortillas or other wraps, then roll up to enclose the filling, place in a lightly greased shallow gratin dish, and sprinkle with ½ cup shredded cheddar cheese. Cook under a preheated hot broiler for 3–4 minutes, until golden and bubbling.

1⏱ Chilled Coconut Soup with Sizzling Shrimp

Serves 2

1¾ cups coconut milk, chilled
⅔ cup chilled plain yogurt
¼ cucumber, finely chopped
3 tablespoons finely chopped
 mint leaves
black pepper
1 tablespoon chopped cilantro
 leaves, to garnish (optional)
naan, to serve

For the shrimp

1 tablespoon sunflower oil
6 oz cooked, peeled jumbo
 shrimp
1 teaspoon minced garlic
½ teaspoon cayenne pepper

- Put the coconut milk, yogurt, cucumber, and mint into a small bowl and mix well, then season with plenty of black pepper. Pour into 2 serving bowls.

- Heat the oil in a skillet until smoking. Toss the shrimp with the garlic and cayenne pepper, then carefully transfer to the hot oil and cook over high heat for 2–3 minutes, until golden in places and sizzling.

- Divide the shrimp between the serving bowls, sprinkle with cilantro, if desired, and serve immediately with naan.

2⏱ Shrimp and Coconut Pan-Fry

Heat 1 tablespoon sunflower oil in a large skillet, add 1 onion, 2 small sliced zucchini, and 1 cored, seeded, and coarsely chopped red bell pepper and stir-fry for 5 minutes. Add 8 oz cooked, peeled jumbo shrimp, ¼ cup coarsely chopped cilantro leaves, and ½ teaspoon each of cayenne pepper, ground coriander, and ground cumin and sauté, stirring, for another 2 minutes. Add ⅔ cup coconut milk, bring to a boil, and serve immediately with rice.

3⏱ Shrimp and Coconut Curry

Heat 1 tablespoon sunflower oil in a saucepan, add 1 thinly sliced onion and 1 thinly sliced garlic clove, and cook for 3 minutes. Add ¼ cup coarsely chopped cilantro leaves and stems and ½ teaspoon each of cayenne pepper, ground coriander, and ground cumin and cook for a few seconds. Pour in 1¾ cups coconut milk and bring to a boil, then reduce the heat, cover, and simmer for 10 minutes. Add 8 oz cooked, peeled jumbo

shrimp and cook for another 5 minutes, until piping hot. Blend 1 teaspoon cornstarch with 1 tablespoon water, then add to the pan and stir well until slightly thickened. Serve with rice.

Pan-Fried Herbed Salmon with Creamy Mascarpone Sauce

Serves 2

2 pieces of salmon fillet, about
    6 oz each, with skin on
1 garlic clove, crushed
⅓ cup chopped parsley, dill,
    and tarragon
1 tablespoon olive oil
1 tablespoon unsalted butter
¼ cup crème fraîche or
    heavy cream
3 tablespoons mascarpone
    cheese
salt and black pepper

- Put the salmon fillets into a bowl with the garlic and 3 tablespoons of the herbs and gently turn to heavily coat in the mixture. Season well.

- Heat the oil and butter in a skillet, add the salmon, and cook over medium-high heat for 3 minutes on each side, until browned and cooked through. Reduce the heat to a gentle simmer and turn the fillets onto the skin side.

- Mix together the crème fraîche or heavy cream, mascarpone, and remaining herbs. Spoon the mixture into the skillet and cook gently for 2–3 minutes, gently stirring around the fish until the sauce is piping hot but not boiling.

- Serve the fish on 2 warm serving plates with the sauce spooned over the top.

 Creamy Salmon with Herbs

Heat 1 tablespoon olive oil in a skillet, add 10 oz cubed skinless salmon fillet, and cook for 4–5 minutes, until cooked through. Add the finely grated rind and juice of 1 lemon, ⅓ cup crème fraîche or heavy cream, and 3 tablespoons mascarpone cheese and heat gently for another 2 minutes. Stir in 3 tablespoons chopped parsley and dill and serve.

 Creamy Salmon with Herbed Mashed Potatoes Put 2 salmon fillets, about 4 oz each, on an aluminum foil-lined broiler rack and cook under a preheated hot broiler for 5 minutes or until opaque and cooked through. Meanwhile, melt 2 tablespoons butter in a saucepan, add 3 tablespoons all-purpose flour, and cook for a few seconds. Remove from the heat and gradually add 1¼ cups milk. Return to the heat and bring to a boil, stirring continuously until boiled and thickened. Add the finely grated rind and juice of 1 lemon, then flake the fish, discarding the skin, and fold in with 4 oz cooked, peeled shrimp. Spoon the mixture into a gratin dish. Mix together 2½ cups cooked mashed potatoes, ¼ cup chopped parsley and dill, and 3 tablespoons mascarpone cheese in a bowl, then spoon the mixture over the seafood. Cook under a preheated medium broiler for 5–10 minutes, until piping hot.

Herbed Cod and Mashed Potatoes with Gruyère and Spinach

Serves 4

4 pieces of skinless cod fillet,
  about 7 oz each
juice of 1 lemon
2 tablespoons olive oil
¼ cup chopped flat leaf parsley
4 slices of prosciutto

For the mashed potatoes

8 russet or Yukon gold potatoes
  (about 2 lb), peeled and cubed
4 tablespoons butter
¼ cup crème fraîche or
  heavy cream
1 cup grated Gruyère cheese
1½ cups baby spinach leaves
salt and black pepper

- Put the cod, lemon juice, oil, and parsley in a large nonmetallic bowl and gently toss to lightly coat. Season with black pepper. Tightly wrap each piece of fish with 1 slice of prosciutto and put on a large baking sheet. Put into a preheated oven, at 425°F, for 12–15 minutes or until cooked through.

- Meanwhile, make the mashed potatoes. Cook the potatoes in a large saucepan of lightly salted boiling water for 15 minutes, until tender. Drain, then return to the pan and mash with the butter and crème fraîche or heavy cream. Fold in the cheese and spinach until the cheese is melted and the spinach wilted, then season. Spoon onto 4 warm serving plates and top with the fish.

Pan-Fried Cod with Herbed Cheese Mashed Potatoes

Heat 2 tablespoons olive oil in a large skillet, add 8 torn slices of prosciutto, and cook over high heat for 2 minutes, until crisp. Remove from the skillet. Heat 2 tablespoons butter in the skillet, add 4 cod fillets, and cook on each side for 3 minutes or until cooked through. Mix 3 cups cooked mashed potatoes with ½ cup grated Gruyère cheese and 2 tablespoons chopped parsley in a microwave-safe bowl and heat in a microwave for 2 minutes. Serve the cod on the potatoes, sprinkled with prosciutto.

Herbed Cod with Cheesy Spinach and Mashed Potato Ramekins

Place 4 cod fillets, about 5 oz each, in a large roasting pan and season well. Sprinkle with ¼ cup chopped parsley. Roast in a preheated oven, at 425°F, for 15–20 minutes or until cooked through. Meanwhile, mix together 3 cups cooked mashed potatoes and 3½ cups spinach leaves in a bowl. Spoon into 4 ramekins and press down firmly. Sprinkle with 1 cup grated Gruyère cheese. Place on the top shelf of the oven for 10–15 minutes, until heated through. Serve with the fish.

Thai Green Fish Curry with Lime Leaves

Serves 4

2 tablespoons vegetable oil

1 large red bell pepper, cored, seeded, and cut into chunks

4 cups snow peas

1 bunch of scallions, coarsely chopped

2 lemon grass stalks, finely chopped

4 lime leaves, finely shredded

1¾ cups coconut milk

3–4 tablespoons Thai green curry paste

12 oz skinless white fish fillets, such as cod, red snapper, or halibut, cubed

5 oz cooked, peeled shrimp

½ cup chopped cilantro leaves

Thai sticky rice, to serve (optional)

- Heat the oil in a large saucepan, add the red bell pepper, and cook for 4 minutes, then add the snow peas, scallions, lemon grass, and lime leaves and cook over medium heat for another 3–4 minutes, until softened.

- Pour in the coconut milk and curry paste and stir well, then simmer gently for 3 minutes. Add the fish and shrimp and continue to cook for 5 minutes, until the fish is opaque and cooked through.

- Stir in the cilantro, then spoon into 4 warm serving bowls and serve with Thai sticky rice, if desired.

 Thai Shrimp Stir-Fry
Heat 2 tablespoons vegetable oil in a large wok, add 2 cored, seeded, and thinly sliced red bell peppers and 4 cups snow peas, and stir-fry for 2 minutes. Add 12 oz cooked, peeled shrimp, 2 teaspoons minced lemon grass, and 2 teaspoons Thai green curry paste and stir-fry for 2 minutes, then add 2½ cups bean sprouts and cook for 1 minute. Add ½ cup coconut milk and heat through until piping hot. Serve with cooked rice, if desired.

Thai-Style Fish Cakes Cook 1 cup jasmine rice in a large saucepan of lightly salted boiling water for 15 minutes, until tender and cooked. Drain well. Meanwhile, place 1 cored, seeded, and finely chopped red bell pepper, ¾ cup finely chopped snow peas, 3 finely chopped scallions, ½ finely chopped lemon grass stalk, 1 finely chopped lime leaf, and 1½ teaspoons Thai green curry paste in a large bowl. Add 9 oz finely chopped skinless white fish fillet, such as cod, red snapper, or halibut, 4 oz coarsely chopped, cooked peeled shrimp, ⅓ cup chopped cilantro leaves, the drained rice, and 2 medium eggs and mix together well. Shape the mixture into 8 small patties. Heat 2 tablespoons vegetable oil in a large skillet, add the patties, and cook over high heat on each side for 2 minutes, until heated through, browned, and a light crust is formed. Serve with a salad.

30 Chile Seafood Stew

Serves 2

2 tablespoons olive oil

1 red onion, cut into thin wedges

1 small red chile, seeded and thinly sliced

1 garlic clove, sliced

2 white round or red-skinned potatoes, peeled and cubed

7 oz prepared squid rings

1 (14½ oz) can diced tomatoes

⅔ cup white wine

3 tablespoons tomato paste

2 tablespoons drained sun-dried tomatoes in oil

2 tablespoons thyme leaves

8 oz fresh mussels

6 oz red snapper fillets, skinned and cut into chunks

warm crusty bread, to serve

- Heat the oil in a large skillet, add the onion, chile, and garlic, and cook over medium heat for 5–8 minutes, until pale brown and softened. Add the potatoes and squid rings and cook for another 2 minutes.

- Add ⅔ cup water, the diced tomatoes, wine, and tomato paste to the skillet and stir well, then add the sun-dried tomatoes and thyme and cook for 8 minutes.

- Meanwhile, wash the mussels under cold running water and discard any that don't shut when tapped. Pull off any fibrous "beards" and remove any barnacles, then rinse again.

- Add the red snapper to the skillet and stir gently through, then add the mussels, cover, and bring to a boil. Cook for 5–7 minutes, shaking the skillet occasionally until the fish is cooked through and the mussels have opened. Discard any that remain closed. Serve with warm crusty bread to mop up the juices.

 Spicy Seafood and Tomato Pan-Fry

Heat 1 tablespoon olive oil in a skillet, add 1 small coarsely chopped onion, and cook for 2 minutes. Add 1 (14½ oz) can diced tomatoes, ½ teaspoon dried red pepper flakes, ⅔ cup white wine, and 10 oz mixed seafood, thawed if frozen, and bring to a boil. Reduce the heat, cover, and simmer for 5 minutes, until piping hot. Serve with crusty bread.

 Spicy Seafood Soup

Heat 2 tablespoons olive oil in a large saucepan, add 1 thinly sliced red onion, ½ small seeded and thinly sliced red chile, and 1 sliced garlic clove, and cook for 3–4 minutes, until softened. Add 7 oz prepared squid rings, 1 (14½ oz) can diced tomatoes, ⅔ cup white wine, 2 tablespoons tomato paste, and 1¼ cups hot fish stock and bring to a boil. Reduce the heat, cover, and simmer for 5 minutes. Meanwhile, wash 8 oz fresh mussels under cold running water and discard any that don't shut when tapped. Pull off any fibrous "beards" and remove any barnacles, then rinse again. Add to the pan and stir well, then cover and cook for 5–7 minutes, until the mussels have opened, discarding any that remain closed. Sprinkle with thyme leaves and serve.

Chile and Lemon Fish Cakes

Serves 2

3 russet or Yukon gold potatoes, peeled and cut into small chunks

8 oz cod

½ cup water

2 tablespoons olive oil

8 scallions, coarsely chopped

½ red chile, seeded and coarsely chopped

finely grated rind of 1 lemon

3 tablespoons chopped parsley

1 egg, beaten

2½ cups ciabatta bread crumbs

⅓ cup vegetable oil

salt and black pepper

To serve

lemon wedges

tartar sauce

- Cook the potatoes in a large saucepan of lightly salted boiling water for 10 minutes, until tender. Drain the potatoes, then return to the pan and mash with a potato masher.

- Meanwhile, place the cod in a small saucepan with the measured water and season well. Bring to a boil, then reduce the heat, cover, and simmer for 5 minutes, until opaque and cooked through. Drain well, then flake.

- Heat the olive oil in a large skillet, add the scallions and chile, and cook over high heat for 2 minutes. Add to the potato mixture. Then add the flaked fish, lemon rind, and parsley and fold through. Shape the mixture into 4 patties.

- Place the beaten egg in a bowl and the bread crumbs in another. Coat the patties in the egg, then the bread crumbs.

- Heat the vegetable oil in a large skillet, add the fish cakes, and cook over high heat for 5–6 minutes, turning, until browned and cooked through. Serve with lemon wedges and tartar sauce.

Chile and Lemon Tuna Balls

Mix together 1½ cups cooked mashed potatoes and 1 (5 oz) can tuna, drained, in a bowl. Heat 1 tablespoon olive oil in a skillet, add 4 chopped scallions and ½ seeded and chopped red chile, and cook for 2 minutes. Fold into the potato mixture with the grated rind of 1 lemon, then shape into 4 rough balls. Heat another 2 tablespoons olive oil in a small skillet, add the tuna balls, and cook over high heat for 3–4 minutes, turning, until hot.

Deep-Fried Chile Cod Balls

Cook 3 peeled and chopped russet or Yukon gold potatoes in a large saucepan of lightly salted boiling water for 10 minutes, until tender. Drain and mash. Put 8 oz cod and ½ cup water in a small saucepan, cover tightly, and cook for 5 minutes, until cooked through. Heat 1 tablespoon olive oil in a small skillet, add 6 finely chopped scallions and ½ small seeded and chopped red chile, and cook for 3 minutes. Flake the fish and add to the mashed potatoes with the scallions and chile. Add the finely grated rind of 1 small lemon. Shape into 8 small balls and roll in 2½ cups fine ciabatta bread crumbs to coat. Fill a deep saucepan halfway with vegetable oil and heat to 375°F or until a cube of bread browns in 30 seconds. Deep-fry the balls in the hot oil for 2–3 minutes, until browned. Remove with a slotted spoon and drain on paper towels. Meanwhile, mix together 1 cup crème fraîche or Greek yogurt, the grated rind of 1 small lemon, and 3 tablespoons chopped parsley in a small bowl. Serve the dip with the fish balls.

30 Roasted Garlicky Herb Sea Bass, Fennel, and Potatoes

Serves 2

2 whole sea bass, about 10 oz each, gutted
1 garlic clove, sliced
¼ cup chopped parsley
2 tablespoons chopped thyme leaves
1 lemon, halved and sliced
1 fennel bulb, trimmed and thinly sliced
3 russet potatoes, cut into thin wedges
1 tablespoon olive oil
salt and black pepper

- Place the fish in a roasting pan and slash both sides deep to the bone. Season well with black pepper.

- Mix together the garlic and herbs in a bowl, then rub the mixture over the fish, pushing it into the slashes. Tuck the lemon slices and fennel under and on top of the fish. Toss the potatoes with the oil and season well, then arrange around the fish.

- Roast in a preheated oven, at 400°F, for 20–25 minutes or until the potatoes are golden and the fish is cooked through.

 Sea Bass Fillets with Garlic and Herb Butter Heat 2 tablespoons butter in a skillet, add 2 sea bass fillets, 3–4 oz each, and cook over medium heat for 2 minutes on each side until cooked through. Add 1 coarsely chopped garlic clove and 1 tablespoon chopped thyme leaves and cook gently for another 1 minute. Serve with microwaved baked potatoes with the herb butter spooned over the top.

 Pan-Fried Herb and Garlic Sea Bass and Fennel Slash 2 gutted sea bass, about 10 oz each, several times on each side and season well. Heat 2 tablespoons butter in a large skillet, add 1 small trimmed and thinly sliced fennel bulb and 1 thinly sliced garlic clove, and cook over medium heat for 3–4 minutes, until slightly softened. Add the fish to the skillet and cook for 4 minutes on each side, or until the flesh is opaque and cooked through. Sprinkle with 1 tablespoon chopped thyme leaves and season well. Serve with crusty bread.

1⃝ Scallop, Bacon, and Pine Nut Pan-Fry

Serves 4

2 tablespoooons butter

10 oz smoked bacon, cut into pieces

12 oz scallops, halved widthwise if large

¼ cup pine nuts

½ cup chopped parsley

finely grated rind of 1 lemon

crusty bread, to serve

- Heat the butter in a large skillet, add the bacon, and cook over high heat for 3 minutes, until browned.

- Add the scallops and pine nuts and cook for 3–4 minutes, until the scallops are cooked through and the pine nuts are browned. Stir in the parsley and lemon rind. Divide the mixture among 4 dishes, spoon any juices over the top, and serve with plenty of crusty bread.

Grilled Scallops in Bacon

Put 16 large scallops, 2 tablespoons chopped parsley, and the finely grated rind of 1 lemon in a bowl and toss well to coat. Wrap 1 bacon strip around each scallop, then secure with toothpicks. Heat 2 tablespoons butter in a ridged grill pan, add the scallops, and cook over high heat for 2 minutes on each side until browned and cooked through. Serve with a simple salad and crusty bread.

Creamy Baked Scallops and Bacon

Heat 2 tablespoons butter in a large skillet, add 8 coarsely chopped bacon strips, and cook over medium heat for 3–4 minutes, until crisp. Add 16 scallops and sauté for 2 minutes. Remove with a slotted spoon and set aside. Add 3 tablespoons all-purpose flour to the skillet and cook for a few seconds, stirring. Remove from the heat and gradually add 1¼ cups milk. Return to the heat and bring to a boil, stirring continuously until boiled and thickened. Return the scallops and bacon to the skillet and fold into the sauce with ½ cup chopped parsley. Spoon into 4 clean and empty scallop shells or ramekins and sprinkle with ½ cup fresh bread crumbs. Bake in a preheated oven, at 375°F, for 10 minutes, until the bread crumbs are golden. Serve with green beans, if desired.

30 Juicy Cod Burgers with Tartar Sauce

Serves 2

3 tablespoons all-purpose flour

2 cod fillets, about 7 oz each

1 egg, beaten

1½ cups fresh whole-wheat bread crumbs

1 tablespoon finely chopped parsley

finely grated rind of ½ lemon

¼ cup sunflower oil

2 good-quality soft wheat buns

2 thick slices of beefsteak tomato

2 handfuls of watercress leaves

salt and black pepper

For the tartar sauce

2 tablespoons crème fraîche or heavy cream

2 tablespoons mayonnaise

1 tablespoon drained and chopped capers

finely grated rind of ½ lemon

- Season the flour on a plate, then toss the cod in the seasoned flour. Place the beaten egg on a second plate, add the fish, and gently coat. Toss the bread crumbs with the parsley and lemon rind, then coat the fish in the bread crumbs.

- Heat the oil in a large skillet, add the coated fish, and cook over medium heat for 2–3 minutes on each side or until golden and cooked through.

- Meanwhile, mix together all the tartar sauce ingredients in a small bowl.

- To assemble the burgers, cut the buns in half. Place 1 tomato slice on each of the bun bottoms, add the hot fish, and top with spoonfuls of the tartar sauce and watercress. Top with the remaining bun halves and serve.

 Cod Buns with Tartar Sauce

Heat 1 tablespoon butter in a skillet, add 2 seasoned cod fillets, about 4 oz each, and cook for 2–3 minutes on each side, or until cooked through. Halve 2 soft buns and place 1 slice of tomato in the bottom of each, then add the fish. Spoon 1 tablespoon of prepared tartar sauce over the top of each. Top with watercress and the remaining bun halves.

20 Fish Stick Buns with Tartar Sauce

Mix together 2 tablespoons each of crème fraîche or Greek yogurt and mayonnaise, 1 tablespoon drained capers, and the finely grated rind of 1 lemon in a small bowl. Season well with black pepper. Cook 6 fish sticks under a preheated medium broiler for 8 minutes, turning once, until browned and cooked through. Cut 2 good-quality soft burger bun in half and place 1 large slice of tomato in the bottom of each, then add 3 fish sticks to each. Spoon on 2 tablespoons of the tartar sauce and put a handful of watercress leaves on top. Top with the remaining bun halves and serve.

 # Asian Shrimp and Crab Stir-Fry

Serves 2

2 tablespoons sesame oil

2 teaspoons peeled and chopped
fresh ginger root

1 (12 oz) package prepared
stir-fry vegetables

1 head of bok choy, halved and
leaves separated

6 oz cooked, peeled jumbo
shrimp

2 oz mixed fresh white and dark
crabmeat

2 tablespoons soy sauce

¼ cup sweet chili sauce

chopped cilantro leaves,
to garnish

· Heat the oil in a large wok or skillet, add the ginger,
and cook for a few seconds. Add the vegetables and
stir-fry for 4 minutes.

· Add the shrimp and cook for 1 minute, then add the
crabmeat and cook and toss over high heat for 2–3 minutes,
until piping hot. Add the soy sauce and chili sauce and
toss again to coat. Serve sprinkled with cilantro.

 ### Gingered Shrimp and Crab Rice

Cook ⅔ cup quick-cooking rice in
a saucepan of boiling water for
10–12 minutes, or according to the
package directions, until tender,
then drain. Meanwhile, heat
2 tablespoons sesame oil in a
skillet, add 2 teaspoons peeled
and chopped fresh ginger root and
1 (12 oz) package prepared stir-fry
vegetables, and stir-fry for 3–4
minutes. Add 6 oz cooked, peeled
jumbo shrimp and 2 oz mixed fresh
white and dark crabmeat and cook
for 3 minutes, until piping hot. Add
the rice, 2 tablespoons soy sauce,
and ¼ cup sweet chili sauce to the
crab mixture. Toss and cook for
2 minutes, until piping hot.

 ### Shrimp and Crab Spring Rolls

Heat 2 tablespoons sesame oil
in a large skillet, add ½ (16 oz)
package prepared stir-fry
vegetables, and cook for
2 minutes. Add 3 oz cooked,
peeled shrimp and continue to
sauté, stirring, for 2 minutes,
until piping hot, then add 2 oz
fresh crabmeat. Remove from
the heat and toss to mix. Add
3 tablespoons sweet chili sauce
and 2 tablespoons chopped
cilantro leaves and toss again.
Place 1 sheet of phyllo pastry
on a board and place
a second sheet on top. Pile
one-quarter of the crab mixture
in the center of the sheets, fold

the sides over the filling, then
fold in each end and roll up to
form a spring roll. Repeat to
make 4 spring rolls. Place on
a baking sheet and bake in a
preheated oven, at 425°F,
for 12–15 minutes, until crisp
and golden.

 # Pan-Fried Prosciutto-Wrapped Salmon

Serves 2

2 skinless salmon fillets, about
  6 oz each
2 tablespoons chopped parsley
2 slices of prosciutto
1 tablespoon olive oil
salt and black pepper

To serve

arugula salad
lemon wedges

- Season the salmon well, then sprinkle with the parsley. Tightly wrap each fillet with 1 slice of prosciutto.

- Heat the oil in a skillet, add the salmon, and cook over medium-high heat for 7–8 minutes, turning occasionally, until browned and cooked through.

- Serve with a arugula salad and lemon wedges.

 Broiled Salmon with Creamy Prosciutto Sauce Heat 1 tablespoon olive oil in a saucepan, add 4 slices of prosciutto, snipped into pieces, and cook for 3–4 minutes, until crisp and browned. Remove with a slotted spoon and set aside. Add 1 tablespoon all-purpose flour to the pan and cook for a few seconds, stirring. Remove from the heat and gradually add 1¼ cups milk. Add 2 cups spinach leaves and ½ teaspoon ground nutmeg and season well with black pepper. Return to the heat and bring to a boil, stirring continuously until boiled, thickened, and the spinach has wilted. Stir in the reserved prosciutto, set aside, and keep warm. Place 2 salmon fillets, about 6 oz each, with skin on, on an aluminum foil-lined broiler rack and season with black pepper. Cook under a preheated hot broiler for 2–3 minutes on each side, or until opaque and cooked through. Serve the salmon with the sauce spooned over the top.

Roasted Prosciutto-Wrapped Salmon and Potatoes Tightly wrap each of 2 skinless salmon fillets, about 6 oz each, with 1 slice of prosciutto. Place in a lightly greased roasting pan. Add 8 new potatoes and season well. Sprinkle with 2 tablespoons chopped parsley and roast in the top of a preheated oven, at 400°F, for 20 minutes or until the fish is cooked through and the potatoes are browned and tender.

QuickCook

Vegetarian

Recipes listed by cooking time

30

20

10

30 Spinach and Feta Phyllo Packages

Serves 2

1 (10 oz) package spinach leaves, rinsed
1 cup crumbled feta cheese
large pinch of freshly grated nutmeg
2 tablespoons chopped parsley
4 sheets of phyllo pastry
¼ cup olive oil
salt and black pepper
tomato and red onion salad, to serve

- Place the spinach in a large saucepan without any extra water, cover, and cook for 2 minutes, until wilted. Drain and squeeze out as much excess water as possible.

- Chop the spinach and mix with the feta, nutmeg, and parsley in a bowl. Season with black pepper (the feta is salty, so check before adding salt).

- Place 2 sheets of phyllo pastry on top of one another and brush lightly with oil. Place half the filling at the end of the sheet, then fold over to make a triangle and continue folding until the filling is enclosed. Brush with oil. Repeat to make 1 more package.

- Place the packages on a baking sheet and bake in a preheated oven, at 400°F, for 15 minutes, until crisp and golden. Serve with tomato and red onion salad.

 1 Spinach and Feta Tortilla Pies

Divide 2 cups baby spinach leaves, 1 cup feta cheese, ½ finely sliced small red onion, and 1 tablespoon chopped parsley between 2 soft flour tortillas, placing the mixture on only one half. Season with a little grated nutmeg and black pepper (the feta is salty, so there's no need to add salt). Fold the tortillas over the filling and press together firmly. Cook in a large skillet for 5–8 minutes, turning once, until the tortillas are crisp and hot. Serve with tomato salad.

 2 Spinach and Feta Salad Tarts

Brush 4 sheets of phyllo pastry with olive oil, cut each sheet in half widthwise, and stack 4 pieces on top of each other at a slight angle to make a star. Repeat with the remaining 4 pieces. Place on a baking sheet and slightly scrunch the edges of the pastry. Brush with olive oil and sprinkle with 2 teaspoons sesame seeds. Bake in a preheated oven, at 400°F, for 10 minutes, until golden. Meanwhile, mix together 2 cups baby spinach leaves, 1 cup crumbled feta cheese, 4 halved cherry tomatoes, 8 pitted ripe black olives, ½ small thinly sliced red onion, and 1 tablespoon chopped parsley in a bowl. Mix with 2 tablespoons French dressing, pile onto the cooked pastry shells, and serve.

MID-VEGE-LAF

30 Pea, Leek, and Potato Soup with Pesto and Cheesy Toasts

Serves 2

1 tablespoon butter

3 white round or red-skinned potatoes, peeled and chopped

1 leek, trimmed, cleaned and sliced

2½ cups hot vegetable stock

1 cup frozen peas

1 tablespoon pesto

salt and black pepper

For the toasts

2 slices of French bread

⅔ cup shredded Gruyère cheese

- Heat the butter in a saucepan, add the potatoes and leek, and cook for 5 minutes to soften. Add the stock and bring to a boil, then reduce the heat, cover, and simmer for 20 minutes, until the potatoes are tender, adding the peas for the final 5 minutes.

- Blend the soup with an immersion blender or in a food processor until smooth. Heat through and season.

- Toast the bread slices on one side under a preheated broiler, then turn the slices over, top with the cheese, and broil until melted.

- Ladle the soup into 2 warm serving bowls, swirl through the pesto, and serve with the toasts.

---

10 Pea and Pesto Soup
Heat 2½ cups frozen peas in 2½ cups vegetable stock in a saucepan. Add 1 crushed garlic clove and simmer for 5 minutes. Blend with an immersion blender, then season and stir in 2 tablespoons crème fraîche or heavy cream and 1 tablespoon pesto. Serve topped with store-bought croutons.

20 Chunky Pea, Leek, and Pesto Soup
Heat 1 tablespoon butter in a saucepan, add 1 trimmed, cleaned, and chopped leek, and cook for 3 minutes, until softened. Add 2½ cups hot vegetable stock, 1 cup frozen peas, 1 cup shredded cabbage, and 2 oz small pasta shapes. Bring to a boil, then reduce the heat, cover, and simmer for 10 minutes, until cooked through. Stir in 1 tablespoon pesto and serve the soup with crusty bread.

30 Curried Cauliflower, Lentils, and Rice

Serves 4

2 tablespoons vegetable oil

1 large onion, sliced

2 teaspoons cumin seeds

2 tablespoons Jalfrezi curry paste

2½ cups cauliflower florets

½ cup red lentils

1 cup basmati rice or other
long-grain rice

3 cups hot vegetable stock

2 carrots, peeled and shredded

½ cup toasted cashew nuts

2 handfuls of cilantro leaves,
to garnish

- Heat the oil in a large saucepan, add the onion, and cook for 5 minutes, until softened. Add the cumin seeds and cook for 30 seconds, then add the curry paste and cook for 30 seconds.

- Add the cauliflower, red lentils, rice, and stock. Bring to a boil, then reduce the heat, cover, and simmer for 10–15 minutes, until cooked through and the liquid has been absorbed.

- Stir in the shredded carrots and heat for 2 minutes, adding a little hot water if the mixture is too dry. Sprinkle with the cashew nuts and serve sprinkled with cilantro leaves.

10 Speedy Cauliflower Pilaf

Heat 2 tablespoons vegetable oil in a large saucepan, add 3 cups white button mushrooms, 2 cups small cauliflower florets, and 2 teaspoons garlic paste, and sauté for 3 minutes, until tender. Add 2 tablespoons medium curry paste, 1¼ cups hot vegetable stock, and ⅔ cup frozen peas and simmer for 2 minutes, then stir in 3 cups cooked long-grain rice and heat through. Stir in 1 (5 oz) package baby spinach leaves until wilted. Sprinkle with ½ cup toasted slivered almonds. Serve with naan and plain yogurt.

20 Easy Cauliflower and Lentil Pilaf

Place 2 tablespoons medium curry paste, 2 tablespoons vegetable oil, and 2 crushed garlic cloves in a large saucepan and sauté for 1 minute. Add 3 cups cauliflower florets, 2 medium chopped zucchini, 3 cups halved white button mushrooms, ½ cup red lentils, 1 cup basmati rice or other long-grain rice, and 3 cups hot vegetable stock and bring to a boil, then reduce the heat, cover, and simmer for 10–15 minutes, until the vegetables are tender and the stock has been absorbed. Stir in 2 coarsely grated carrots and ½ cup toasted cashew nuts. Serve on warm chapattis with spoonfuls of plain yogurt.

30 Falafels with Beet Salad and Mint Yogurt

Serves 2

1 (15 oz) can chickpeas, rinsed and drained

½ small red onion, coarsely chopped

1 garlic clove, chopped

½ red chile, seeded

1 teaspoon ground cumin

1 teaspoon ground coriander

handful of flat leaf parsley

2 tablespoons olive oil

salt and black pepper

For the beet salad

1 carrot, shredded

1 raw beet, shredded

2 cups baby spinach leaves

1 tablespoon lemon juice

2 tablespoons olive oil

For the mint yogurt

⅔ cup Greek-style plain yogurt

1 tablespoon chopped mint leaves

½ garlic clove, crushed

- To make the falafels, place the chickpeas, onion, garlic, chile, cumin, coriander, and parsley in a food processor. Season, then blend to make a coarse paste. Shape the mixture into 8 patties and set aside.

- To make the salad, place the carrot, beet, and spinach in a bowl. Season, add the lemon juice and oil, and stir well.

- To make the mint yogurt, mix together all the ingredients and season with a little salt.

- Heat the oil in a skillet, add the falafels, and sauté for 4–5 minutes on each side until golden. Serve with the beet salad and mint yogurt.

---

10 Falafel and Beet Pita Pockets

Warm 4 prepared falafels in a preheated oven, at 375°F, for 5 minutes, adding 2 pita breads for 2 minutes. Split open the pitas, then fill each with a small handful of watercress, some cooked fresh beet slices, tomato slices, and the falafels. Add a spoonful of plain yogurt with a little chopped cucumber to each pita and serve.

20 Chickpea Burgers with Beet

Put 1 (15 oz) can chickpeas, rinsed and drained, 1 garlic clove, 1 teaspoon harissa paste or ½ teaspoon chili powder, and a small handful of flat leaf parsley in a food processor. Season, then blend to make a coarse paste. Shape the mixture into 4 patties. Heat 2 tablespoons olive oil in a skillet, add the patties, and sauté for 4–5 minutes, turning once, until browned and heated through. Serve on toasted burger buns with spinach leaves, a spoonful of yogurt with some chopped cucumber, and some chopped cooked fresh beet. (If you don't want to cook all the burgers, they can be frozen.)

30 Baked Cheesy Zucchini

Serves 2

1 tablespoon olive oil
2 zucchini, chopped
1 garlic clove, crushed
4 scallions, chopped
2 eggs
⅔ cup light cream
1 teaspoon whole-grain mustard
1 cup shredded sharp cheddar
   cheese
¼ cup fresh white bread crumbs
1 tablespoon chopped parsley
salt and black pepper

- Heat the oil in a skillet, add the zucchini, garlic, and scallions, and sauté for 5 minutes, until the zucchini are browned and just tender. Divide the mixture between 2 individual ovenproof dishes.

- Beat together the eggs, cream, and mustard in a small bowl, then season. Stir in half the cheese and pour the mixture over the zucchini.

- Mix together the remaining cheese, the bread crumbs, and parsley in a bowl. Season and sprinkle the mixture over the eggs. Bake in a preheated oven, at 400°F, for 20 minutes, until the tops are golden and the egg mixture has just set.

---

10 Zucchini and Cheddar Omelet

Heat 1 tablespoon olive oil in a flameproof skillet, add 2 chopped zucchini and 1 crushed garlic clove, and sauté for 3 minutes, until tender. Beat together 6 eggs, 1 tablespoon water, and 1 teaspoon whole-grain mustard in a small bowl, then season. Stir in ½ cup shredded sharp cheddar cheese, then pour over the zucchini. Cook for 2–3 minutes, until the bottom is browned and set. Sprinkle with another ¼ cup shredded cheddar, then put the skillet under a preheated medium broiler for 2 minutes, until the top is set and golden. Cut into wedges to serve.

20 Cheesy Zucchini Carbonara

Cook 6 oz spaghetti in a saucepan of lightly salted boiling water for 10 minutes, or according to the package directions, until just tender. Meanwhile, heat 1 tablespoon olive oil in a skillet, add 2 zucchini, cut into thin sticks, 1 crushed garlic clove, and 4 scallions, cut into thin sticks, and sauté for 3–4 minutes, until browned and tender. Beat together 2 eggs, ⅔ cup light cream, and ½ cup grated Parmesan cheese in a small bowl, then season. Drain the spaghetti, add to the zucchini, and pour over the beaten eggs.

Mix well and gently heat through, being careful not to scramble the eggs. Serve with extra grated Parmesan and a grinding of black pepper.

20 Corn Fritters with Sweet Chili Dip

Serves 4

2 cups all-purpose flour

2 eggs

½ cup milk

6 scallions, chopped

2 (11 oz) cans corn kernels, drained

2 tablespoons vegetable oil, plus extra if needed

salt and black pepper

cilantro leaves, to garnish

For the dip

1 cup light cottage cheese

2 tablespoons sweet chili sauce

- Place the flour in a bowl and make a well in the center. Break the eggs into the well and add the milk. Gradually whisk the flour into the eggs and milk to make a smooth, thick batter. Stir in the scallions and corn kernels and season.

- Heat the oil in a large skillet, add spoonfuls of the batter, about 4 at a time, to the pan, and cook for 2 minutes on each side until browned and firm to the touch. Remove from the skillet and repeat with the remaining batter, adding extra oil, if necessary.

- Meanwhile, make the dip. Stir the cottage cheese in a bowl to soften, then lightly stir through the sweet chili sauce to form a marbled effect. Serve the fritters with the dip, sprinkled with cilantro leaves.

---

10 Spicy Corn Fondue

Bring 1¼ cups dry white wine to a boil in a large saucepan, then reduce the heat and add 2 cups each of grated Gruyère cheese and Swiss cheese, a handful at a time, stirring until melted. Blend 2 teaspoons cornstarch with 4 teaspoons cold water, then add to the pan and stir until thickened. Add 1 (15¼ oz) can corn kernels, drained, 2 large pinches of cayenne pepper, and salt and black pepper. Serve hot with tortilla chips for dipping.

30 Corn Hash Browns with Spicy Salsa

Parboil 6 halved white round or red-skinned potatoes in a large saucepan of lightly salted boiling water for 10 minutes. Meanwhile, make the salsa. Chop 4 tomatoes and mix with 1 seeded and finely chopped red chile and 2 tablespoons chopped flat leaf parsley. Season, then add 2 tablespoons olive oil and 2 teaspoons balsamic vinegar. Set aside. Drain the potatoes and cool slightly. Coarsely grate the potatoes into a bowl and add 1 (15¼ oz) can corn kernels, drained, 4 chopped scallions, 2 cups shredded Swiss cheese or Gruyère cheese, and 2 beaten eggs. Season and mix lightly, then shape the mixture into 8 cakes. Heat 2 tablespoons olive oil in a large skillet, add the cakes, and cook for 5–8 minutes, until crisp and golden, turning once. Serve with the spicy salsa.

30 Stuffed Pasta, Pine Nut, and Butternut Gratin

Serves 2

¼ butternut squash, peeled, seeded, and sliced
1 tablespoon olive oil
2 garlic cloves, unpeeled
3 tablespoons pine nuts
1 (8 oz) package fresh four cheese tortelloni
⅔ cup heavy cream
¼ cup grated Parmesan cheese
¼ cup fresh white bread crumbs
4 sage leaves
salt and black pepper
arugula and tomato salad, to serve (optional)

- Place the squash on a baking sheet, drizzle with the oil, and season. Roast in a preheated oven, at 400°F, for 5 minutes. Add the garlic and pine nuts, return to the oven, and cook for another 15–20 minutes, until the squash is tender, the garlic is soft and the pine nuts are toasted.

- Toward the end of the cooking time, cook the tortelloni in a saucepan of lightly salted boiling water for 3–4 minutes, or according to the package directions, until tender. Drain, transfer to a flameproof dish with the roasted squash and pine nuts, and gently toss together.

- Squeeze the soft garlic from its skin, mix with the cream, and season. Spoon the sauce over the tortelloni and squash and sprinkle with the Parmesan, bread crumbs, and sage leaves. Place under a preheated medium broiler for 2–3 minutes, until golden and bubbling. Serve with a arugula and tomato salad, if desired.

 Creamy Pumpkin and Pine Nut Stuffed Pasta Cook 1 (8 oz) package fresh pumpkin and pine nut pasta in a saucepan of lightly salted boiling water for 3–4 minutes, or according to the package directions, until tender. Meanwhile, in another saucepan, heat ⅔ cup heavy cream and 1 crushed garlic clove. Season and stir in 2 cups baby spinach leaves. Drain the pasta and mix with the sauce. Serve sprinkled with grated Parmesan cheese.

 Creamy Squash, Pine Nuts, and Stuffed Pasta Cook ¼ peeled, seeded, and chopped butternut squash in a saucepan of lightly salted boiling water for 10 minutes, until tender. Heat 1 tablespoon olive oil in a skillet. Drain the squash, add to the skillet, and cook for 5 minutes, stirring occasionally until golden. Add 1 crushed garlic clove, 3 tablespoons pine nuts, and 4 sage leaves and cook for 2 minutes.

Meanwhile, in a separate saucepan, cook 1 (8 oz) package fresh spinach and ricotta tortelloni in lightly salted boiling water for 3–4 minutes, or according to the package directions, until tender, then drain and add to the squash with ⅔ cup heavy cream. Heat through for 2 minutes until bubbling, season, and serve sprinkled with grated Parmesan cheese.

Spiced Butternut Squash Soup

Serves 4

½ butternut squash,
  peeled and chopped
2 parsnips, peeled and chopped
½ celeriac, peeled and chopped
2 teaspoons ground cumin
2 teaspoons ginger paste from
  a jar or tube
5 cups hot vegetable stock
¼ cup crème fraîche or
  Greek yogurt
salt and black pepper
flat leaf parsley, to garnish

- Place the vegetables, spices, and stock in a large saucepan. Bring to a boil, then reduce the heat, cover, and simmer for 15 minutes, until tender. Blend with an immersion blender until almost smooth and season.

- Ladle the soup into 4 warm serving bowls and add a spoonful of crème fraîche or Greek yogurt to each one. Serve sprinkled with flat leaf parsley.

 Butternut Soup with Roasted Peppers Heat 2 tablespoons olive oil in a large saucepan, add 1 teaspoon cumin seeds, and sauté until they start "popping." Add 2 (14½ oz) cans butternut squash soup and 1 cup drained, chopped roasted peppers from a jar. Heat through and serve topped with spoonfuls of crème fraîche or Greek yogurt and a sprinkle of smoked paprika.

 Roasted Butternut and Red Pepper Soup Put ½ peeled, seeded, and chopped butternut squash, 2 cored, seeded, and chopped red bell peppers, and 2 chopped onions in a large roasting pan. Drizzle with 2 tablespoons olive oil, sprinkle with 2 teaspoons cumin seeds and season. Roast in a preheated oven, at 425°F, for 20 minutes, until tender, adding 2 chopped garlic cloves for the final 5 minutes. Transfer the vegetables into a large saucepan and add 5 cups hot vegetable stock, bring to a boil, then reduce the heat and simmer for 5 minutes. Blend with an immersion blender until almost smooth. Serve topped with spoonfuls of crème fraîche or Greek yogurt and sprinkled with flat leaf parsley.

30 Garlic and Herb Mushroom Tart

Serves 2

2 tablespoons butter

1 garlic clove, crushed

2 cups halved button mushrooms

2 tablespoons chopped parsley

1 teaspoon thyme leaves

½ sheet of ready-to-bake
rolled dough piecrust

½ cup ricotta cheese

1 tablespoon tomato paste

beaten egg, to glaze

½ cup grated manchego cheese
or pecorino Romano cheese

salt and black pepper

- Heat the butter in a skillet, add the garlic and mushrooms, and cook for 3–5 minutes, stirring, until browned. Add the parsley and thyme and season. Remove from the heat.

- Place the dough on a baking sheet. Mix together the ricotta and tomato paste and spread over the dough, leaving a 1 inch border around the edge. Top with the mushroom mixture.

- Brush the border with a little beaten egg. Fold the border up over the edge of the filling, loosely scrunching or folding it as you go around. Brush the dough with the beaten egg and sprinkle the grated cheese over the filling and pastry.

- Bake in a preheated oven, at 400°F, for 15 minutes, until the pastry is golden.

---

1 **Garlic and Herb Mushrooms with Hash Browns** Heat 2 tablespoons garlic and herb butter in a skillet, add 3 cups button mushrooms, and cook for 3 minutes. Add ½ cup chopped sun-dried tomatoes and ¼ cup crème fraîche or sour cream and season. Heat through, adding a little milk if the sauce is too thick. Heat 2 store-bought hash browns in a toaster or under a preheated broiler, spoon the mushroom mixture over the potatoes, and serve sprinkled with sliced manchego cheese and chopped parsley.

2 **Garlic, Herb, and Brie Stuffed Mushrooms** Heat 4 tablespoons butter in a skillet, add the chopped stems from 4 large portobello mushrooms and 1 crushed garlic clove, and cook for 2 minutes. Stir in 1 tablespoon chopped parsley and 1 teaspoon chopped thyme leaves and season. Place the mushrooms on a baking sheet, stem side up. Spoon the garlic and herb mixture onto the mushrooms. Top each with 1 tablespoon tomato and basil pasta sauce, 2 halved cherry tomatoes, and 1 oz chopped brie. Bake in a preheated oven, at

400°F, for 15 minutes, until the mushrooms are tender. Sprinkle with a little extra chopped parsley and serve with crusty bread to mop up the juices.

Mediterranean Tomato Soup

Serves 2

3 tomatoes, coarsely chopped
⅓ cup olive oil
1 garlic clove, crushed
1¼ cups hot vegetable stock
1 tablespoon tomato paste
½ teaspoon granulated sugar
1 teaspoon oregano leaves,
  plus extra leaves to garnish
1 tablespoon shredded
  basil leaves
1 ciabatta roll, torn into pieces
2 tablespoons grated Parmesan
  cheese
salt and black pepper

- Place the tomatoes in a saucepan with 2 tablespoons of the oil and the garlic. Cook for 3 minutes, until softened, then add the stock, tomato paste, sugar, oregano, and shredded basil. Bring to a boil, then reduce the heat, cover, and simmer for 10 minutes.

- Meanwhile, spread the ciabatta pieces over a baking sheet and drizzle with 2 tablespoons of the oil. Toast under a preheated medium broiler for a few minutes, turning occasionally, until crisp and golden.

- Blend the soup with an immersion blender until smooth. Stir in half the Parmesan and season.

- Ladle the soup into 2 warm serving bowls, drizzle with the remaining oil, and top with some of the ciabatta croutons. Sprinkle with the remaining Parmesan and a few oregano leaves. Serve with the remaining croutons.

 Easy Tomato and Basil Soup

Put 3 tomatoes, 1 peeled garlic clove, ⅔ cup tomato puree or tomato sauce, 2 slices of ciabatta bread, crusts removed, 2 tablespoons pesto, 1 tablespoon olive oil, 1 teaspoon white wine vinegar, and a pinch of granulated sugar in a food processor. Blend until smooth, then pour into a saucepan and heat through for 3–4 minutes, until piping hot. Season, then serve with ciabatta toast.

 Tomato and Bean Soup

Heat 1 tablespoon olive oil in a saucepan, add 1 small chopped onion, 1 peeled and chopped carrot, and ½ chopped zucchini and cook for 5 minutes. Add 1¼ cups tomato puree or tomato sauce and 1¼ cups hot vegetable stock and bring to a boil, then reduce the heat and simmer for 20 minutes, until the vegetables are tender, adding 1 cup shredded curly kale for the final 5 minutes. Stir in 1 cup rinsed and drained canned cannellini beans and 1 tablespoon shredded basil leaves and heat through. Season and serve with crusty bread.

MID-VEGE-KEU

Tomato and Mozzarella Sourdough Bruschetta

Serves 2

2 thick slices of sourdough bread
¼ cup olive oil
½ teaspoon salt flakes
1 small red onion, cut into thin wedges
½ teaspoon cumin seeds
8 baby plum tomatoes, halved
4 oz mozzarella pearls, drained
1 tablespoon chopped cilantro leaves, to garnish

- Lightly brush each of the sourdough slices with oil, sprinkle with the salt flakes, and toast under a preheated hot broiler for 30 seconds–1 minute on each side, until golden.

- Meanwhile, heat the remaining oil in a skillet, add the onion and cumin seeds, and cook over medium heat for 5 minutes, stirring occasionally, until browned and softened.

- Add the tomatoes and cook for another 1 minute, being careful not to let them lose their shape. Add the mozzarella and remove the pan from the heat, shaking it a little to warm the cheese very slightly.

- Divide the mixture between the toasts and serve sprinkled with the cilantro.

Warm Tomato and Mozzarella Salad with Sourdough Croutons Put 8 halved cherry tomatoes and 5 oz thinly sliced mozzarella cheese in a bowl. Heat 2 tablespoons olive oil in a skillet, add 1 thinly sliced red onion and 1 teaspoon cumin seeds, and cook over medium heat for 5 minutes, until browned and softened. Add the onion mixture to the mozzarella and tomatoes, tossing until all the ingredients are slightly warmed. Arrange on 2 serving plates. Heat 2 tablespoons olive oil in a small skillet, add 1 cubed slice of sourdough bread, and sauté over high heat for 1 minute, turning frequently, until browned. Sprinkle with the salad to serve.

Baked Tomato and Mozzarella Sourdough Bread Drizzle 4 thin slices of sourdough bread with ¼ cup olive oil. Heat 1 tablespoon olive oil in a skillet, add 1 small thinly sliced onion and 1 teaspoon cumin seeds, and cook over medium heat for 3 minutes, stirring occasionally, until browned and softened. In a lightly greased small, shallow ovenproof dish, layer the bread slices with 4 thinly sliced tomatoes, the warm onions, and 5 oz thinly sliced mozzarella cheese, finishing with a layer of cheese. Bake in a preheated oven, at 400°F, for 15 minutes, until golden and hot.

 # Chickpea, Artichoke, and Tomato Pan-Fry

Serves 4

2 (15 oz) can chickpeas, rinsed and drained

2 (14 oz) can artichokes, drained and halved

⅓ cup olive oil

1 bunch of scallions, coarsely chopped

2 teaspoons ground cumin

3 fresh tomatoes, cut into thin wedges

12 sun-dried tomatoes in oil, drained, plus 2 tablespoons of the oil

3 tablespoons mixed fresh herbs

black pepper

To serve

3 tablespoons grated Parmesan cheese

warm crusty bread

- Place the chickpeas in a bowl and lightly crush with a potato masher. Season well with black pepper.

- Place the artichokes on an aluminum foil-lined broiler rack and drizzle with 2 tablespoons of the olive oil. Cook under a preheated hot broiler for 5 minutes, until lightly charred in places. Set aside.

- Heat the remaining oil in a large skillet, add the scallions, cumin, fresh tomatoes, and chickpeas and cook over high heat for 5 minutes, then add the sun-dried tomatoes and oil, herbs, and artichokes and toss well.

- Serve in 4 warm serving bowls with the Parmesan sprinkled over the top and warm crusty bread to mop up the juices.

 Rustic Chickpea and Tomato Dip

Put 2 (15 oz) cans chickpeas, rinsed and drained, ½ cup olive oil, 8 coarsely chopped scallions, 12 sun-dried tomatoes in oil, drained, plus 2 tablespoons of the oil, ¼ cup snipped chives, and ¼ cup chopped basil leaves in a food processor. Season well and process until almost smooth but still textured. Serve with vegetable sticks and breadsticks.

 Warm Chickpea, Artichoke, and Tomato Stew Heat 2 tablespoons olive oil in a large saucepan, add 1 large coarsely chopped onion, 2 teaspoons ground cumin, 2 teaspoons ground coriander, and 1 teaspoon ground paprika, and cook for 3 minutes, then add 2 (5 oz) cans chickpeas, rinsed and drained, 2 (14 oz) cans artichokes, drained, 3 fresh tomatoes, cut into thin wedges, 2½ cups hot vegetable stock, and 12 drained and coarsely chopped sun-dried tomatoes in oil. Bring to a boil, then reduce the heat, cover, and simmer for 20 minutes, stirring occasionally. Season well and serve.

30 Asparagus, Eggplant, Brie, and Tomato Quiche

Serves 2

½ sheet of ready-to-bake rolled dough piecrust

¼ cup olive oil

½ small eggplant, cubed

8 asparagus spears, trimmed and cut into 2 inch lengths

4 oz brie, cut into chunks

6 sun-dried tomatoes in oil, drained

½ cup milk

3 eggs

2 tablespoons chopped thyme leaves

salt and black pepper

simple dressed salad, to serve

- Use the dough to line a 12 x 6 inch fluted tart pan and trim the edges. Chill in the refrigerator.

- Heat the oil in a large skillet, add the eggplant, and cook over high heat for 5 minutes, until browned and soft, then add the asparagus and cook for another 2 minutes, until a little browned.

- Arrange the brie, tomatoes, eggplant, and asparagus in the dough-lined pan. Mix together the milk, eggs, and thyme in a small bowl, season well, and pour into the pastry shell.

- Place in the top of a preheated oven, at 425°F, for 20 minutes, until golden and set. Serve warm with a simple dressed salad.

10 Eggplant, Brie, and Tomato Melted

Stacks Cut 1 small eggplant into ¼ inch slices. Heat ⅓ cup olive oil in a large skillet, add all the eggplant slices, and cook for 2 minutes on each side, until golden and soft. On an aluminum foil-lined broiler rack, layer the slices with 4 oz sliced brie and 8 drained sun-dried tomatoes in oil to form 2 stacks, finishing with a slice of brie. Cook under a preheated hot broiler for about 1 minute, until the cheese has melted and the stacks are warm. Serve with a simple salad.

20 Asparagus, Eggplant, Brie, and Tomato Tortilla

Heat ¼ cup olive oil in a large, flameproof skillet, add ½ small cubed eggplant, and cook over high heat for 5 minutes, until golden and soft. Add 8 asparagus spears, trimmed and cut into 2 inch lengths, and cook for another 3 minutes, then add 6 drained and coarsely chopped sun-dried tomatoes in oil and stir well. Remove from the heat. In a small bowl, beat together 5 eggs and ⅓ cup milk and season well. Add 2 tablespoons chopped thyme leaves and beat again. Pour the egg mixture into the skillet and mix well to evenly distribute the vegetables, then sprinkle with 3 oz cubed brie. Return to the heat and cook gently for 5 minutes, until the bottom is set, then place the skillet under a preheated hot broiler and cook for 4–5 minutes, until golden and set. Serve in wedges with a simple dressed salad.

Warm Spinach and Feta Tortilla Slices

Serves 2

3 tablespoons olive oil
1 small red onion, thinly sliced
1 garlic clove, coarsely chopped
1 (8 oz) package spinach leaves
1⅓ cups crumbled feta cheese
¼ cup mascarpone cheese
1 tablespoon sunflower oil
2 large soft flour tortillas
2 tablespoons grated
   Parmesan cheese
salt and black pepper

- Heat the olive oil in a large, flameproof skillet, add the onion and garlic, and cook over medium-high heat for 3–4 minutes, until browned and softened. Add the spinach and stir well for 1–2 minutes, until wilted.

- Drain off any excess juices from the skillet and transfer the spinach mixture to a bowl. Stir in the feta and mascarpone and season well.

- Rinse out the skillet and add the sunflower oil. Place a tortilla in the pan and evenly spoon the spinach mixture over the tortilla, then place the second tortilla on top. Press down well, then sprinkle with the Parmesan.

- Put the skillet over the heat and cook for 2–3 minutes, then place under a preheated hot broiler and cook for 2 minutes, until browned and the cheese has melted. Serve cut into wedges.

Simple Spinach and Feta Wraps

Heat 3 tablespoons olive oil in a small skillet, add 1 small thinly sliced red onion, and cook over medium heat for 3–4 minutes, until softened. Transfer to a bowl and stir in 1½ cups shredded spinach leaves and 1⅓ cups crumbled feta cheese. Put 2 soft flour tortillas on a board and spread each with 1 tablespoon a condiment of your choice, then add the spinach and feta mixture. Roll up the tortillas tightly and cut in half to serve.

Spinach and Feta Burritos

Heat 2 tablespoons olive oil in a skillet, add 1 thinly sliced red onion and 1 coarsely chopped garlic clove, and cook over medium heat for 3 minutes until browned and softened. Add 1 (8 oz) package spinach leaves and cook, stirring and tossing, for 2–3 minutes, until wilted. Remove from the heat and add 3 tablespoons mascarpone cheese and 1⅓ cups crumbled feta cheese and mix well. Divide the filling evenly between 2 soft flour tortillas, make 1 or 2 folds to enclose the filling and place in a shallow ovenproof dish. Sprinkle with ¾ cup shredded sharp cheddar cheese and bake in a preheated oven, at 400°F, for 15 minutes, until melted and pale golden. Serve with a simple salad.

1 ⏱ Spinach Tortelloni, Walnut, and Blue Cheese Gratin

Serves 2

1 (9 oz) pack fresh spinach and
  ricotta tortelloni
1½ cups prepared cheese sauce
1 teaspoon ground nutmeg
1 cup fresh whole-wheat
  bread crumbs
½ cup coarsely chopped walnuts
½ cup finely crumbled
  blue cheese
simple salad, to serve

- Cook the tortelloni in a large saucepan of lightly salted boiling water for 3 minutes, or according to the package directions. Drain well, then return to the pan. Add the cheese sauce and ground nutmeg and heat through.

- Transfer to a shallow gratin dish and level the top. Mix the bread crumbs with the walnuts and blue cheese, then sprinkle it over the pasta.

- Cook under a preheated hot broiler for 2–3 minutes, until the top is golden and melted. Serve with a simple salad.

---

2 Blue Cheese, Spinach, and Walnut Tart

Put ½ sheet of ready-to-bake rolled dough piecrust on a baking sheet, lift up the 4 corners, and pinch together to form a shell, then lightly prick with a fork. Place in a preheated oven, at 400°F, for 12–15 minutes, until golden. Meanwhile, heat 1 tablespoon olive oil in a skillet, add 1 small thinly sliced onion, and cook for 3–4 minutes, until softened, then add 1 (6 oz) package spinach leaves and ½ teaspoon ground nutmeg. Fill the shell with the spinach mixture and ½ cup crumbled blue cheese, then top with 1 tablespoon finely chopped walnuts. Return to the oven for 2–3 minutes. Serve in slices.

3 Blue Cheese, Spinach, and Walnut Gnocchi Casserole

Heat 2 tablespoons butter in a saucepan, add ½ cup coarsely chopped walnuts, and cook over medium heat for 2 minutes, until turning brown, then add 3 tablespoons all-purpose flour and cook for 30 seconds, stirring. Remove from the heat and gradually add 1¼ cups milk. Return to the heat, add 1 teaspoon ground nutmeg, and bring to a boil, stirring continuously until boiled and thickened. Remove from the heat, add 1 (5 oz) package baby spinach leaves and ⅔ cup crumbled blue cheese, and stir well until the spinach is wilted and the cheese is melted.

Meanwhile, cook 1 (9 oz) package fresh gnocchi in a saucepan of lightly salted boiling water for 3 minutes, or according to the directions instructions. Drain well, then add to the pan and stir to coat. Transfer to a shallow ovenproof dish and sprinkle with 3 tablespoons grated Parmesan cheese. Place at the top of a preheated oven, at 425°F, for 15 minutes, until bubbling. Serve with a simple salad and crusty bread, if desired.

3 Pea, Parmesan, and Mint Risotto

Serves 2

2 tablespoons olive oil
1 onion, thinly sliced
1 cup risotto rice
2½ cups hot vegetable stock
⅓ cup grated Parmesan cheese
1 cup frozen peas
3 tablespoons chopped mint
  leaves
½ Boston lettuce, thinly shredded
salt and black pepper
warm crusty bread, to serve

- Heat the oil in a skillet, add the onion, and cook over medium heat for 3 minutes, until softened. Add the rice and cook, stirring, for 2 minutes.

- Pour in all the stock and bring to a boil, then reduce the heat, cover, and simmer gently for 15 minutes, until the rice is tender, stirring occasionally and adding a little more water, if necessary.

- Add the Parmesan, peas, and mint and cook for another 3 minutes, until the peas have defrosted. Stir in the shredded lettuce and stir well, then season well. Serve with warm crusty bread.

1 Pea, Feta, and Mint Pilaf

Heat 2 cups cooked long-grain rice until heated through, or prepare 1 (9 oz) package precooked rice according to the package directions . Meanwhile, heat 2 tablespoons olive oil in a skillet, add 1 small thinly sliced onion, and cook for 3–4 minutes, until softened. Add 1 cup frozen peas and ¼ cup water and cook for 2 minutes, until hot, then add the rice and crumble in 1⅓ cups feta cheese and 2 tablespoons chopped mint leaves. Toss well and serve.

2 Cheesy Pea and Mint Rice Balls

Put ½ cup cream cheese and 2 cups cooked long-grain rice or 1 (9 oz) package precooked rice in a bowl and mix well. Add 1 egg yolk, ½ cup defrosted peas, 1 tablespoon chopped mint leaves, and season well. Mix well until firm, then shape into 8 balls. Roll in 1 cup fresh white bread crumbs to lightly coat. Heat 2 tablespoons olive oil in a skillet, add the balls, and cook for 3–4 minutes, turning frequently, until browned. Serve hot with a simple salad.

30 Goat Cheese and Butternut Squash Stuffed Peppers

Serves 2

2 tablespoons olive oil

2 red bell peppers, halved, cored, and seeded

¼ butternut squash, peeled, seeded, and cut into small chunks

1 small red onion, coarsely chopped

2 tablespoons black olive tapenade (paste)

3 oz soft goat cheese, crumbled

2 tablespoons fresh bread crumbs

1 tablespoon grated Parmesan cheese

To serve

simple salad

crusty bread (optional)

- Heat 1 tablespoon of the oil in a large skillet, add the bell peppers, cut side down, and cook for 2 minutes, then turn the bell peppers over and cook for another 2 minutes. Remove from the skillet.

- Meanwhile, heat the remaining oil in a separate saucepan, add the squash and onion, and cook for 5 minutes, until slightly softened. Remove from the pan and toss with the tapenade in a bowl, then add the goat cheese and gently toss together.

- Spoon the mixture into the bell pepper halves, then place the peppers in a roasting pan and sprinkle with the bread crumbs and Parmesan.

- Place in a preheated oven, at 400°F, for 15 minutes, until the tops are browned and cooked through. Serve hot with a simple salad and crusty bread, if desired.

 Red Pepper and Goat Cheese Bruschetta Heat 3 tablespoons olive oil in a skillet, add 1 small thinly sliced red onion and 1 cored, seeded, and coarsely chopped red bell pepper, and cook for 5 minutes. Meanwhile, lightly toast 2 slices of soda bread until crisp, then spread each with 1 tablespoon black olive tapenade (paste). Top with the red pepper mixture, arrange 4 oz soft rind goat cheese on top, and serve.

 Red Pepper, Butternut, and Goat Cheese Soup Heat 2 tablespoons olive oil in a skillet, add 1 cored, seeded, and coarsely chopped red bell pepper and ¼ peeled and seeded butternut squash, cut into pieces, and cook for 10 minutes, until softened and browned in places. Place in a food processor with 1¼ cups hot chicken stock and 4 oz soft goat cheese and process until smooth. Season well and serve.

Tempura Mixed Vegetables with Chili Sauce

Serves 4

vegetable oil, for deep-frying
1 large red bell pepper, cored,
    seeded, and cut into chunks
12 baby corn
2 cups broccoli florets
8 asparagus spears, trimmed
6 large scallions, cut into
    2 inch lengths
chili dipping sauce, to serve

For the batter

3 tablespoons all-purpose flour
⅓ cup cornstarch
2 eggs, beaten
⅓ cup beer
salt

- Sift the flour and cornstarch into a bowl and season with a little salt. Make a well in the center, add the eggs, and whisk a little, then gradually add the beer, pouring it in slowly and whisking continuously to make a smooth batter.

- Fill a deep saucepan halfway with vegetable oil and heat to 375°F, or until a cube of bread browns in 30 seconds. Working quickly, dip the vegetable pieces, one by one, into the batter. Deep-fry in batches in the hot oil for 1–2 minutes, until lightly browned. Remove with a slotted spoon, drain on paper towels, and keep warm. Serve with chili dipping sauce.

---

10 Sweet Chili Vegetable Stir-Fry

Heat 3 tablespoons sesame oil in a large wok or skillet, add 1 cored, seeded, and coarsely chopped red bell pepper, 16 baby corn, halved lengthwise, and 1½ cups small broccoli florets, and stir-fry over high heat for 3 minutes. Add 12 coarsely chopped scallions and 12 asparagus spears, trimmed and cut into 2 inch lengths, and stir-fry for another 3 minutes, until tender and lightly charred in places. Add ⅓ cup sweet chili sauce and 3 tablespoons soy sauce and cook for 1 minute, stirring continuously until piping hot. Serve with cooked rice, if desired.

30 Sweet Chili and Tempura Vegetable Noodles Cook the Tempura Mixed Vegetables as above. Meanwhile, cook 8 oz soba noodles and 1½ cups trimmed fine green beans in a saucepan of lightly salted boiling water for 10 minutes, until tender. Drain well. In a large wok or skillet, toss the tempura with the noodles and beans. Mix together ½ cup sweet chili sauce, 3 tablespoons soy sauce, and 3 tablespoons sesame oil in a small bowl, then toss into the noodles. Serve hot.

20 Red Lentils with Naan

Serves 4

2 tablespoons peanut oil

2 large onions, thinly sliced

1 red bell pepper, cored, seeded, and sliced

4 tomatoes, coarsely chopped

2 garlic cloves, coarsely chopped

4 teaspoons curry powder

2 teaspoons turmeric

1½ cups red lentils

3¾ cups hot vegetable stock

4 mini naans

salt and black pepper

coarsely chopped cilantro leaves, to garnish

plain yogurt, to serve

- Heat the oil in a large skillet, add the onions and red bell pepper, and cook over medium heat for 3 minutes, until starting to soften. Add the tomatoes and garlic and cook for another 2 minutes, then add the curry powder, turmeric, and lentils and stir well.

- Pour in the stock and bring to a boil. Reduce the heat, cover, and simmer gently for 15 minutes, until the lentils are completely cooked through and soft, adding a little more water, if necessary. Season well.

- Meanwhile, heat the naans in a preheated oven, at 350°F, for 5–8 minutes, or until warm.

- Spoon the dahl onto the warm naans, sprinkle with chopped cilantro, and serve with spoonfuls of yogurt.

---

10 Speedy Chickpea Dahl

Heat 2 tablespoons peanut oil in a large saucepan, add 1 chopped onion, and cook over medium heat for 3 minutes, then add 2 teaspoons curry powder and 1 teaspoon turmeric. Stir in 2 (15 oz) cans chickpeas, rinsed and drained. Remove from the heat and mash the chickpeas with a potato masher, breaking them up well. Pour in 2½ cups hot vegetable stock and bring to a boil, then reduce the heat, cover, and simmer for 3 minutes. Serve with naans and chopped cilantro leaves.

30 Yellow Lentil Dahl

Heat 2 tablespoons peanut oil in a large skillet, add 2 large coarsely chopped onions, and cook over medium heat for 3 minutes, until slightly softened. Add 2 teaspoons cumin seeds, 4 teaspoons curry powder, 2 teaspoons turmeric, and 4 coarsely chopped tomatoes and cook for 1 minute, then add 1½ cups yellow lentils. Stir in 3¾ cups hot vegetable stock and bring to a boil, then reduce the heat, cover, and simmer for 25 minutes, adding 2 handfuls of fresh spinach leaves for the final 3 minutes. Add a little water if it is too dry. Serve with warm naans and spoonfuls of plain yogurt.

Roasted Pepper, Caper, and Spinach Pappardelle Gratins

Serves 4

12 oz pappardelle
1 red bell pepper, cored, seeded, and cut into chunks
1 yellow bell pepper, cored, seeded, and cut into chunks
2 tablespoons olive oil
1 cup coarsely chopped, pitted ripe black olives
¼ cup drained capers
1½ (5 oz) packages baby spinach leaves
10 oz mozzarella cheese, cubed
¼ cup grated Parmesan cheese

- Cook the pappardelle in a large saucepan of lightly salted boiling water for 8–10 minutes, or according to the package directions, until just tender.

- Meanwhile, put the bell peppers in a roasting pan and toss with the oil. Cook under a preheated hot broiler for 5 minutes, turning until lightly charred and soft.

- Drain the pasta and return to the pan with the olives, capers, spinach, and mozzarella and toss over low heat for 1 minute, until the spinach wilts and the mozzarella starts to melt. Add the roasted bell peppers with the oil and toss.

- Pile into 4 flameproof serving bowls and sprinkle each with Parmesan, then place under a preheated hot broiler for 1 minute until the tops are golden. Serve hot.

Roasted Pepper, Caper, and Spinach Pasta Cook 1¼ lb fresh pasta in a large saucepan of lightly salted boiling water for 3 minutes or according to the package directions. Drain well, then add 2 (7 oz) jars roasted peppers, drained, ¾ cup chopped, pitted ripe black olives, and ¼ cup drained capers. Toss well and heat for 2 minutes, until piping hot. Season well and serve with 2 handfuls of baby spinach leaves stirred through.

Baked Roasted Pepper, Caper, and Spinach Penne Core, seed, and cut 2 red bell peppers and 2 yellow bell peppers into chunks, then toss with 2 tablespoons olive oil. Cook under a preheated hot broiler for 5 minutes, until lightly charred and softened. Meanwhile, cook 12 oz penne in a large saucepan of lightly salted boiling water for 8–10 minutes, or according to the package directions, until just tender. Drain, then return to the pan and toss with the roasted peppers and ¾ cup coarsely chopped, pitted ripe black olives, 1½ (5 oz) packages baby spinach leaves, and ¼ cup drained capers. Transfer to a large, shallow gratin dish and top with 10 oz thinly sliced mozzarella cheese. Sprinkle with ½ cup fresh bread crumbs and place at the top of a preheated oven, at 425°F, for 15 minutes, until golden and bubbling. Serve with a simple green salad.

1⃝ Harissa Eggplant and Hummus Flatbreads

Serves 2

1 small eggplant, cut into
small cubes

1 tablespoon harissa paste

¼ cup olive oil

2 soft flatbreads or chapattis

⅓ cup store-bought hummus

2 cups arugula leaves

¼ cup chopped cilantro leaves

- Place the eggplant and harissa in a bowl and toss to lightly coat. Heat the oil in a large skillet, add the eggplant, and cook over medium-high heat for 5–7 minutes, until softened and cooked through.

- Meanwhile, warm the flatbreads in a microwave for 30 seconds. Place on 2 warm serving plates and spread with the hummus. Top with the eggplant, then sprinkle with the arugula and cilantro and serve.

 Harissa Eggplant and Chickpea Flatbreads Heat ¼ cup olive oil in a large skillet, add 1 small sliced eggplant and 1 small thinly sliced red onion, and cook over high heat for 5 minutes, until softened. Add 1 tablespoon harissa paste, 1 teaspoon ground coriander, and 1 (15 oz) can chickpeas, rinsed and drained, and cook over medium heat for another 2 minutes, until hot. Stir in ¾ cup canned diced tomatoes, cover, and cook for 5 minutes, until the sauce is thick and pulpy. Season well, then sprinkle with 3 tablespoons chopped cilantro leaves. Spoon onto 2 warm flatbreads and roll up to serve, if desired.

 Harissa Eggplant and Chickpea Dip with Flatbread Chips Cut 3 flatbreads into triangles, lightly brush each with a little olive oil, and sprinkle each with a few salt flakes. Place on a baking sheet and bake in a preheated oven, at 400°F, for 5–6 minutes, until golden. Let cool. Meanwhile, heat ¼ cup olive oil in a large skillet, add 1 small cubed eggplant and 1 coarsely chopped red onion, and cook over medium-high heat for 5 minutes. Add 1 tablespoon harissa paste and cook for another 1 minute. Transfer the mixture to a food processor, add the finely grated rind and juice of 1 lemon and 1 teaspoon ground coriander, and process until smooth. Return to the pan, add 1 (15 oz) can chickpeas, rinsed and drained, and stir for 2 minutes, until piping hot. Serve the warm dip sprinkled with chopped cilantro leaves, with the chips.

30 Roasted Carrot and Beet Pearl Barley with Feta

Serves 4

2 red onions, cut into thin wedges

16 bunched carrots, scrubbed and cut into chunks

1 large raw beet, peeled, and cut into thin wedges

olive oil

1½ teaspoons cumin seeds

1½ teaspoons ground coriander

1½ chicken bouillon cubes

1⅓ cups pearl barley

2 cups crumbled feta cheese

⅓ cup cilantro leaves

- Place all the prepared vegetables in a large roasting pan, drizzle with the oil, and toss to coat. Add the cumin seeds and ground coriander and toss again. Place at the top of a preheated oven, at 425°F, for 20–25 minutes, until the vegetables are tender and lightly charred in places.

- Meanwhile, bring a large saucepan of lightly salted water to a boil, add the bouillon cubes and pearl barley, and cook for 20 minutes, until the grain is tender. Drain, then toss with the vegetables. Add the crumbled feta and cilantro leaves, toss well, and serve.

---

10 Carrot and Beet Couscous with Feta

Put 1¼ cups couscous in a heatproof bowl and just cover with boiling water. Cover with plastic wrap and let stand for 5 minutes. Meanwhile, heat 3 tablespoons olive oil in a large skillet, add 6 peeled and thinly sliced carrots, and cook for 5 minutes, stirring frequently, until softened. Add 1½ teaspoons cumin seeds and ¾ teaspoon ground coriander and cook for another 1 minute, then add the couscous, 6 cooked fresh beets, coarsely chopped, and a handful of arugula leaves. Toss together, then serve topped with 2 cups crumbled feta cheese.

20 Carrot, Beet, and Feta Gratin

Heat 3 tablespoons olive oil in a large skillet, add 1 large thinly sliced red onion, 8 peeled and sliced carrots, and 4 raw beets, peeled and cut into thin wedges, and cook for 8–10 minutes, until tender and cooked through. Add 1½ teaspoons cumin seeds and ¾ teaspoon ground coriander, then toss and cook for another 2 minutes. Divide among 4 small gratin dishes, then sprinkle 2 cups crumbled feta cheese over the tops. Cook under a preheated hot broiler for 2–3 minutes, until the feta has browned in places. Serve with warm crusty bread.

Pan-Cooked Eggs with Spinach and Leeks

Serves 2

2 tablespoons butter
1 leek, trimmed, cleaned,
    and thinly sliced
¼ teaspoon dried
    red pepper flakes
2 (5 oz) packages baby
    spinach leaves
2 eggs
3 tablespoons plain yogurt
pinch of ground paprika
salt and black pepper

- Heat the butter in a skillet, add the leek and red pepper flakes, and cook over medium-high heat for 4–5 minutes, until softened. Add the spinach and season well, then toss and cook for 2 minutes, until wilted.

- Make 2 wells in the center of the vegetables and break the eggs into the well. Cook over low heat for 2–3 minutes, until the eggs are set. Spoon the yogurt on top and sprinkle with the paprika.

Leek and Spinach Omelet

Heat 1 tablespoon olive oil in a large skillet, add 1 small trimmed, cleaned, and thinly sliced leek, and cook over medium heat for 3–4 minutes, then add 1 (6 oz) package baby spinach leaves and cook for 2 minutes, stirring, until wilted. In a small bowl, beat together 4 eggs and season well, then pour the eggs over the spinach mixture. Cook over low heat for 2–3 minutes, until the bottom is set, then place a baking sheet over the top of the pan and cook for another 1 minute, until the top is set. Gently flip one side of the omelet over onto the other, then cut the omelet in half. Lightly toast 2 pieces of walnut bread and spread each with 1 tablespoon tomato chutney, then place an omelet half over each.

Baked Spinach and Leek Frittata

Beat 5 eggs in a small bowl and season well. Heat 2 tablespoons butter in a skillet, add 1 trimmed, cleaned, and thinly sliced leek, and cook over medium heat for 3 minutes, then add 2 (5 oz) packages baby spinach leaves and cook for 2 minutes, stirring continuously until wilted. Spoon into a shallow ovenproof dish and pour the eggs over the top. Bake in a preheated oven, at 425°F, for 20 minutes, until browned and set. Serve in wedges, sprinkled with paprika.

30 Mozzarella, Tomato, and Basil Thin-Crust Pizza

Serves 2

1 (6½ oz) package pizza crust mix
all-purpose flour, for dusting
¼ cup tomato paste or sun-dried
tomato pesto
1 tablespoon chopped basil leaves
1 beefsteak tomato, sliced
5 oz mozzarella cheese, sliced
1 tablespoon drained capers or
caperberries
olive oil, for drizzling
salt and black pepper

- Put the pizza crust mix into a bowl and prepare according to the package directions. Roll out the dough on a lightly floured surface to a circle about 10 inches in diameter, and place on a nonstick baking sheet.

- Put the paste or pesto in a small bowl and add the chopped basil. Spread over the pizza crust, leaving a 1 inch border around the edge. Arrange the tomato and mozzarella slices over the top and sprinkle with the capers in the gaps between. Season well.

- Place in the top of a preheated oven, at 425°F, for 15–20 minutes, until browned and cooked. Drizzle with oil and serve cut into wedges.

 Herbed Mozzarella and Tomato Naan Pizza Spread 1 large naan with ¼ cup spicy tomato relish. Arrange 1 small sliced beefsteak tomato and 5 oz mozzarella cheese slices over the top. Sprinkle with ½ teaspoon lightly crushed coriander seeds, then cook under a preheated hot broiler for 3–4 minutes, until golden and melted. Sprinkle with 2 tablespoons chopped cilantro leaves, halve, and serve.

Mozzarella, Tomato, and Basil Salad with Dough Balls Prepare 1 (6½ oz) package pizza crust mix according to the package directions, adding 1 tablespoon tomato paste or sun-dried pesto to the dried mix and reducing the measured water by 2 tablespoons. Mix to a smooth dough, then shape into 8 balls. Place on a nonstick baking sheet and bake in a preheated oven, at 425°F, for 12 minutes, until browned and cooked through. Meanwhile, put 1 sliced beefsteak tomato, 5 oz thinly sliced mozzarella cheese, 1 tablespoon drained capers, and 3 tablespoons shredded basil leaves in a bowl. Add 2 tablespoons olive oil, then season well and toss together. Arrange on 2 serving plates and serve with the hot dough balls.

QuickCook
Desserts

Recipes listed by cooking time

30

20

10

Baked Honeyed Figs and Raspberries

Serves 4

8 figs, quartered
1¼ cups raspberries
¼ cup honey
finely grated rind of
  1 medium orange
coconut ice cream, to serve

- Cut 4 large squares of aluminum foil. Divide the figs and raspberries among the pieces of foil, drizzle the honey over the berries, and sprinkle with the orange rind.

- Bring the edges of the foil up to the center and twist to form packages. Put onto a large baking sheet and bake in a preheated oven, at 400°F, for 15 minutes.

- Open the packages and serve the fruit and juices with spoonfuls of coconut ice cream.

 Fig, Raspberry, and Honey Yogurt Desserts Crumble 8 gingersnaps among 4 glasses. Divide 4 chopped figs and 1 cup raspberries among the glasses and drizzle each with honey. Spoon 3 tablespoons coconut yogurt over each and serve each topped with a raspberry.

 Fig, Raspberry, and Honey Brûlées Divide 6 chopped figs among 4 heatproof ramekins, then add ½ cup raspberries, ½ teaspoon finely grated orange rind, and ½ teaspoon honey to each. Divide 1⅔ cups plain Greek yogurt over the tops and spread evenly to cover. Put ¾ cup granulated sugar into a saucepan with 1 tablespoon water and cook over low heat, without stirring, for about 5 minutes, until the sugar melts and turns a rich caramel color. Gently tip the pan occasionally to avoid hot spots. Quickly pour the caramel over the yogurt, then let cool and set for 10 minutes.

Speedy Iced Tiramisu

Serves 2

8 ladyfingers, halved
¼ cup strong black coffee
4 scoops of vanilla ice cream
1 oz semisweet chocolate, grated

- Divide the ladyfingers between 2 serving plates or shallow bowls, then drizzle with the coffee.

- Top each with 2 scoops of the ice cream and sprinkle the grated chocolate on top. Serve immediately.

---

2 Cappuccino Fudge Creams

Mix ½ teaspoon coffee granules with 2 tablespoons boiling water, then let cool slightly. Beat together ¾ cup mascarpone cheese and 1 tablespoon sugar in a bowl. Lightly stir in the coffee and spoon the mixture into 2 glasses. Top each with a spoonful of whipped cream, then cover and chill in the refrigerator for 10 minutes. Sprinkle 1 oz chopped fudge over the top and serve with ladyfingers.

3 Tiramisu

Mix together ¼ cup strong black coffee and 1 tablespoon coffee liqueur in a small bowl. Put 4 ladyfingers into a shallow dish and pour half the coffee mixture over the sponges. In a separate bowl, mix together ⅔ cup mascarpone cheese and 3 tablespoons confectioners' sugar. Lightly whip ½ cup heavy cream and fold into the mascarpone. Spoon half the mixture over the ladyfingers and spread evenly.

Sift 1 teaspoon unsweetened cocoa powder over the top. Repeat the layers and dust cocoa powder over the top. Cover and chill for 10 minutes.

30 Roasted Plum and Orange Compote with Granola

Serves 4

8 plums, halved and pitted

juice and finely grated rind of
1 medium orange

⅓ cup demerara sugar or
other raw sugar

½ teaspoon ground cinnamon

1 stick butter

½ cup rolled oats

¼ cup coarsely chopped
hazelnuts

plain yogurt, to serve

- Place the plums in a shallow roasting pan or baking dish. Add the orange rind and juice and sprinkle with ¼ cup of the sugar and the cinnamon. Dot half the butter on top and roast in a preheated oven, at 400°F, for 20 minutes, spooning over the juices halfway through, until the plums have softened.

- Meanwhile, line a large baking sheet with aluminum foil, then sprinkle with the oats, hazelnuts, and remaining sugar. Dot with the remaining butter and place in the oven with the plums for 5–10 minutes, until lightly browned and toasted, stirring once to coat in the melted butter.

- Spoon the compote into 4 serving dishes, sprinkle with the crunchy oat granola, and serve with yogurt.

 Simple Pan-Fried Orangey Plums

Heat 2 tablespoons butter in a skillet, add 8 halved, pitted, and quartered plums, and sauté in the butter for 5 minutes, until soft. Stir in the grated rind of 1 orange and ¼ cup demerara or other raw sugar. Sprinkle with a few roasted chopped hazelnuts and serve with whipped cream.

 Plum and Orange Whip

Put 8 halved and pitted plums and the juice and grated rind of 1 orange in a saucepan and cook for 2–3 minutes. Add ¼ cup demerara or other raw sugar and 1 teaspoon ground cinnamon and cook for 5 minutes, until the plums are tender. Blend with an immersion bender until almost smooth, then pour into a shallow dish and let cool for 10 minutes. Meanwhile, whip ⅔ cup heavy cream until just thick enough to form soft peaks, then fold in 1¼ cups prepared vanilla pudding. Stir in the plum puree to create a marbled effect. Sprinkle with roasted chopped hazelnuts and serve.

3O Crushed Strawberry and Lime Shortbreads

Serves 4

1 stick butter
¼ cup superfine sugar or
  granulated sugar, plus
  1 teaspoon
1¼ cup all-purpose flour
finely grated rind of 1 lime
⅓ cup heavy cream
3 strawberries, hulled and
  chopped
confectioners' sugar, for dusting

- Line a baking sheet with parchment paper. Put the butter, ¼ cup of the superfine or granulated sugar, the flour, and most of the lime rind (reserving a little for decoration) in a food processor and pulse until the mixture comes together to form a dough.

- Divide the mixture into 8 equal pieces and roll each piece into a ball. Place on the prepared baking sheet and flatten the cookies with the back of a fork.

- Bake in a preheated oven, at 350°F, for 10–15 minutes, until lightly browned. Transfer to a wire rack to cool.

- While the cookies are cooling, whip the cream with the remaining sugar, then fold in the strawberries.

- Sandwich together 2 cookies with some strawberry cream, then repeat with 6 more cookies. Decorate with lime rind and a dusting of confectioners' sugar. Serve any remaining strawberry cream separately.

 1O Strawberry and Lime Brandy Snap Baskets Warm 2 tablespoons strawberry preserves to soften. Let cool slightly, then stir in 8 hulled and sliced strawberries to coat in the preserves. Place 2 tablespoons ricotta cream in each of 4 store-bought brandy snap baskets, sprinkle with a little grated lime rind, and spoon the strawberries over the top.

 2O Strawberry and Lime Cookie Stacks Whip together 1 cup heavy cream, the finely grated rind of 1 lime and 2 teaspoons superfine or granulated sugar in a bowl. Hull and slice 1 cup strawberries. Layer 12 store-bought thin plain cookies with spoonfuls of the lime cream and the sliced strawberries to form 4 stacks of 3 cookies each.

10 Caramelized Berry Rice Pudding

Serves 2

1 cup frozen mixed berries, such as rasberries, blueberries, and hulled strawberries, halved or quartered if large

1 tablespoon granulated sugar

1½ cups prepared rice pudding

¼ cup plain yogurt

1 tablespoon packed light brown sugar

- Put the fruit into a saucepan with the granulated sugar and heat, stirring, for 3–4 minutes, until the fruit has softened and defrosted. Transfer the fruit and juice to a flameproof dish.

- Mix together the rice pudding and yogurt in a bowl, then spoon the fruit over the top. Sprinkle with the brown sugar and place under a preheated hot broiler for about 2 minutes, until the sugar starts to melt and caramelize. Cool slightly before serving.

---

20 Rice Pudding Berry Meringue

Heat 1 cup frozen mixed berries with 1 tablespoon granulated sugar in a saucepan for a few minutes, until defrosted and juicy. Arrange 6 ladyfingers in a shallow flameproof dish and pour the warm fruit over the top. Heat 1½ cups prepared rice pudding in a microwave on Medium for 2 minutes, until warm. Pour it over the fruit. In a clean bowl, whisk 1 egg white using a handheld electric mixer until just stiff, then add 2 tablespoons superfine sugar, whisking well between each addition, until firm and glossy. Spoon the meringue over the rice pudding, swirling with the back of a spoon. Place under a preheated medium broiler for 3–4 minutes, until the meringue is golden.

30 Caramelized Rice Pudding with

Warm Berries Gently simmer 1¼ cups milk and 2 tablespoons short-grain rice in a saucepan for 20–25 minutes, stirring occasionally, until the milk has been absorbed and the rice is tender. Stir in 2 teaspoons granulated sugar and a few drops of vanilla extract. Spoon the rice into a small flameproof dish, sprinkle with 1 tablespoon packed light brown sugar, and place under a preheated hot broiler for 2 minutes, until the sugar melts and caramelizes. Meanwhile, heat 1 cup frozen mixed berries with 1 tablespoon granulated sugar in a saucepan for a few minutes, until defrosted and juicy. Cool the rice pudding slightly, then serve with the warm fruit.

 # Pan-Fried Caramel Apples

Serves 4

6 tablespoons butter

4 sweet crisp apples, such as
Pippin or Golden Delicious,
cored and cut into wedges

⅓ cup firmly packed light
brown sugar

⅓ cup heavy cream

- Heat the butter in a large skillet, add the apple wedges, and sauté for 5 minutes, until soft and lightly browned. Remove from the skillet and set aside.

- Add the sugar to the butter and juices in the pan and heat gently, stirring to dissolve the sugar. Simmer for 1 minute, then stir in the cream and heat through for 1 minute.

- Return the apples to the pan and coat in the caramel sauce. Cool slightly, then serve.

 **Caramel Apple
Pecan Waffles**

Heat 2 tablespoons butter in a large skillet, add 4 peeled and cored sweet, crisp apples, cut into wedges, and sauté over a gentle heat for 3–4 minutes, until soft and lightly browned. Stir in ½ cup caramel sauce, such as dulce de leche, and a few pecan halves and heat through for 1 minute. Serve on toasted waffles.

 **Warm Apple Cakes
with Caramel**

Sauce Put ⅓ cup all-purpose flour, ¼ teaspoon baking powder, ¼ cup firmly packed light brown sugar, ¼ cup soft margarine, and 1 egg in a food processor. Blend until soft and smooth. Stir in ½ peeled, cored, and chopped sweet, crisp apple. Spoon the batter into 4 cups of a muffin pan lined with paper muffin liners. Bake in a preheated

oven, at 350°F, for 15 minutes, until risen and firm to the touch. Meanwhile, melt 4 tablespoons butter and ¼ cup packed light brown sugar in a saucepan. Bring to a boil, then stir in ⅔ cup heavy cream. Simmer and stir to make a smooth caramel sauce. Remove the cakes from the paper liners and serve with the slightly cooled caramel sauce.

Molten Chocolate Lava Cakes

Serves 2

6 tablespoons butter, plus extra
  for greasing
⅓ cup superfine sugar or
  granulated sugar
3 oz semisweet chocolate,
  broken into pieces
2 medium eggs
3 tablespoons all-purpose flour

To serve

cream
raspberries

- Grease 2 individual ovenproof ramekins and sprinkle
  with 1 teaspoon of the sugar.

- Melt together the chocolate and butter in a microwave-safe
  bowl in a microwave on Medium, checking every minute
  until melted and smooth.

- Whisk together the eggs and remaining sugar with a
  handheld electric mixer until thick, pale, and creamy. Whisk
  in the melted chocolate mixture, then lightly fold in the flour.

- Spoon the mixture into the prepared ramekins and place on
  a baking sheet. Bake in a preheated oven, at 375°F, for
  15–20 minutes, until firm on the outside but still wobbly in
  the center.

- Turn out the cakes into 2 serving bowls and serve warm with
  cream and raspberries.

---

1 **Chocolate Muffins
with Pudding** Heat
⅔ cup prepared vanilla pudding
in a small saucepan, then stir in
1 tablespoon chocolate hazelnut
spread. Warm 2 chocolate
muffins in a microwave on
Medium for 30 seconds, then
serve with the chocolate
pudding spooned over the top.

2 **Warm Chocolate
Croissant Dessert**
Halve 2 croissants and spread
each with 1 tablespoon chocolate
spread. Cut into thick slices and
place in a shallow ovenproof
dish. Beat together 1 egg, ⅔ cup
milk, and 1 tablespoon granulated
sugar in a small bowl, then pour
over the croissants. Bake in a

preheated oven, at 375°F,
for 15 minutes, until the custard
has just set. Sprinkle with
1 shaved chocolate bar and
serve with cream.

30 Berry and White Chocolate Tarts

Serves 2

1 sheet store-bought
   rolled dough piecrust
all-purpose flour, for dusting
2 oz white chocolate, broken into
   pieces
⅓ cup mascarpone cheese
2 tablespoons light cream
⅔ cup mixed blackberries
   and raspberries
white chocolate shavings,
   to decorate
confectioners' sugar, for dusting

- Roll out the dough on a lightly floured surface, then cut out 2 circles and use to line two 4 inch tart pans, trimming off any excess. Prick the bottoms with a fork and line with parchment paper and pie weights or dried beans.

- Place the pans on a baking sheet and bake in a preheated oven, at 375°F, for 10 minutes. Remove the paper and weights and return to the oven for another 5 minutes, until the pastry is crisp and golden. Let cool.

- Meanwhile, melt the white chocolate in a microwave-safe bowl in a microwave on Medium, checking every 30 seconds, until melted and smooth, being careful not to let it overheat.

- Beat together the mascarpone and cream in a bowl until smooth, then beat in the melted chocolate. Spoon the mixture into the shells, then top with the fruit and some white chocolate shavings. Dust with confectioners' sugar and serve.

 Iced Berries with Hot White Chocolate Sauce Put 1½ cups frozen mixed berries onto a microwave-safe plate, then place in a microwave on Defrost for 1 minute, until just starting to soften. Divide between 2 glasses or dishes. Melt together 3 oz chopped white chocolate, broken into pieces, and ½ cup heavy cream in a microwave-safe bowl in a microwave on Medium, checking every 30 seconds, until melted and smooth. Pour the warm sauce over the fruit and serve immediately.

 White Chocolate and Blackberry Turnovers Cut 1 sheet of ready-to-bake puff pastry into two 6 inch squares. Divide ½ cup blackberries and 2 oz chopped white chocolate between the squares. Brush the edges with a little beaten egg and fold the pastry over the filling to make triangles. Press the edges firmly with the back of a fork to seal. Place the turnovers on a baking sheet, brush with beaten egg, and sprinkle with a little granulated sugar. Bake in a preheated oven, at 400°F, for 15 minutes, until well risen and golden.

30 Lemon Polenta Cake with Vanilla Strawberries

Serves 4

6 tablespoons butter, softened, plus extra for greasing

¾ cup superfine sugar or granulated sugar

1 egg

⅓ cup ricotta cheese

¼ cup ground almonds (almond meal)

3 tablespoons polenta or cornmeal

½ teaspoon baking powder

grated rind of 1 lemon

¼ cup water

½ teaspoon vanilla extract

½ cup hulled and halved strawberries

- Grease a 6 inch cake pan and line the bottom with parchment paper. In a bowl, beat together the butter, ⅓ cup of the sugar, the egg, ricotta, ground almonds, polenta, baking powder, and lemon rind, using a handheld electric mixer, until smooth.

- Spoon the batter into the prepared pan and level the surface. Bake in a preheated oven, at 375°F, for 20 minutes, until golden and firm to the touch.

- Meanwhile, place the remaining sugar in a saucepan with the measured water and heat, stirring, to dissolve the sugar. Simmer for 3 minutes, until syrupy. Cool slightly, then stir in the vanilla bean extract.

- Remove the cake from the pan and cut into wedges (any extra cake can be frozen). Mix the strawberries with the vanilla syrup and spoon over the cake to serve.

 Lemon Cake and Strawberry Trifle

Spread 4 slices of store-bought pound cake with 2 tablespoons lemon curd. Cut into cubes and place in a dish or 4 glasses with 8 hulled and chopped strawberries. Mix together a 1¼ cups prepared vanilla pudding and 2 tablespoons lemon curd in a separate bowl, then spoon over the cake and strawberries. Top with ¼ cup extra thick heavy cream. Sprinkle with a few chopped pistachio nuts and serve.

 Lemon Merinuge with Strawberries

Lightly whip 1¼ cups heavy cream in a bowl until just thick enough to form soft peaks. Break 4 meringue nests into pieces and add to the bowl with ⅔ cup hulled and chopped strawberries. Lightly fold into the cream with 2 tablespoons lemon curd. Spoon into 4 glasses and top each with 1 teaspoon lemon curd and ½ hulled strawberry.

Blueberry and Banana French Toast

Serves 4

2 eggs
¼ cup milk
4 teaspoons granulated sugar
4 slices of crusty white bread
4 tablespoons butter
½ cup blueberries
2 bananas, sliced

To serve
ice cream
maple syrup

- Beat together the eggs, milk, and 2 teaspoons of the sugar in a small bowl. Pour into a shallow dish and dip both sides of the bread slices into the egg mixture.

- Heat the butter in a large skillet, add the bread (you might need to cook 1 slice at a time), and cook for 2 minutes on each side, until crisp and golden. Sprinkle the remaining sugar on top.

- Cut the French toasts in half diagonally and sprinkle with the blueberries and banana slices. Serve with ice cream and a drizzle of maple syrup.

---

10 **Blueberry Pancakes with Banana**

Mix together ⅔ cup all-purpose flour, ½ teaspoon baking powder, 1 tablespoon sugar, 1 egg, and ⅓ cup milk to make a smooth, thick batter. Stir in ¼ cup blueberries. Heat 1 tablespoon sunflower oil in a large skillet, add 2 large spoonfuls of the batter, and cook for 1–2 minutes on each side, until lightly browned. Repeat with the remaining batter to make 2 more pancakes. Serve warm with sliced banana and a drizzle of honey.

30 **Banana and Blueberry Custard Tarts** Unroll 1 sheet of store-bought rolled dough piecrust and cut out circles large enough to line four 4 inch tart pans. Slice 1 large banana and place the slices over the pastry shell bottoms with a few blueberries. Beat together 2 eggs, ½ cup light cream, and 2 tablespoons superfine or granulated sugar in a small bowl, then pour the mixture into the pastry shells. Bake in a preheated oven, at 375°F, for 20 minutes, until the pastry is cooked and the filling is just set. Dust with confectioners' sugar and serve with a few extra blueberries.

Spiced Pan-Fried Pineapple with Rum

Serves 2

2 tablespoons butter

4 prepared fresh pineapple wedges, skin removed, or canned slices

¼ cup firmly packed light brown sugar

1 piece of preserved ginger from a jar, chopped

2 tablespoons preserved ginger syrup from the jar

2 tablespoons raisins

¼ cup rum

coconut ice cream, to serve

- Heat the butter in a skillet, add the pineapple, and cook over high heat for 2 minutes, until starting to brown. Reduce the heat, add the sugar, ginger, ginger syrup, and raisins and simmer for 1 minute, until the sugar has dissolved.

- Add the rum and cook for 2 minutes, until the sauce is syrupy. Serve warm with scoops of coconut ice cream.

Upside-Down Pineapple and Rum Tart

Heat ¼ cup prepared caramel sauce, such as dulce de leche, in an ovenproof 6 inch skillet. Add a dash of rum and stir well. Cut 3 drained canned pineapple slices in half, place in the skillet in a single layer and heat through. Unroll 1 sheet of ready-to-bake puff pastry and cut out an 8 inch circle. Remove the skillet from the heat and place the pastry over the fruit, tucking in the edges. Place in a preheated oven, at 400°F, for 15 minutes, until lightly browned and well risen. Turn out onto a plate, being careful because the juices will be hot. Serve warm with ice cream.

Pineapple Fritters with Rum Sauce

Heat 2 tablespoons butter and ¼ cup packed light brown sugar in a saucepan, stirring to dissolve the sugar. Drain 1 (8 oz) can pineapple slices, reserving the juice, then add 3 tablespoons of the juice to the pan and simmer for 2 minutes. Add a splash of rum and remove from the heat. Whisk together ⅔ cup all-purpose flour, 1 egg plus 1 egg yolk, and ⅓ cup milk in a bowl to make a batter. In a clean bowl, whisk 1 egg white until just stiff, then fold into the batter. Pat the pineapple slices dry on paper towels, then dip in the batter, one at a time, to coat. Heat about 1 inch vegetable oil in a large skillet until hot, then sauté the pineapple slices for a few minutes until crisp and golden. Remove with a slotted spoon and place on a plate with 2 tablespoons superfine or granulated sugar mixed with a large pinch of ground cinnamon. Turn the fritters in the sugar to coat. Warm the rum sauce and serve with the fritters.

Grilled Fruit Packages with Pistachio Yogurt

Serves 2

1 cup mixed blueberries and raspberries

2 peaches or nectarines, halved, pitted, and sliced

½ cinnamon stick, halved

1 tablespoon honey

2 tablespoons orange juice

3 tablespoons chopped shelled pistachio nuts, plus extra to decorate

¼ cup plain Greek yogurt

- Cut 2 large, double thickness squares of aluminum foil. Divide the fruit and cinnamon between the squares and drizzle the honey and orange juice over the fruit. Fold the foil over the filling and scrunch the edges to seal.

- Place the packages on a barbecue grill or under a preheated medium broiler for about 10 minutes, until the fruit is soft and hot.

- Open the packages and transfer the fruit to serving bowls. Mix together the pistachios and yogurt in a bowl. Serve with an extra sprinkling of pistachios and spoon the yogurt over the warm fruit.

 Warm Fruit and Pistachio Compote

Put 1 cup mixed blueberries and raspberries, 1 halved, pitted, and chopped peach, 1 tablespoon honey, 2 tablespoons orange juice, and ½ cinnamon stick in a saucepan, then simmer gently for 5 minutes. Sprinkle with chopped pistachio nuts and serve with amaretti cookies and Greek yogurt.

 Phyllo Fruit Pies with Pistachio

Yogurt Cut 2 sheets of phyllo pastry into six 6 inch squares. Melt 2 tablespoons butter and brush some of it over each square. Place 3 squares on top of each other to make 2 stacks. Divide 1 halved, pitted, and chopped peach, ¼ cup blueberries, and ¼ cup raspberries between the squares, then sprinkle with a pinch of ground cinnamon and the grated rind of ½ orange. Gather the phyllo pastry up over the filling and scrunch at the top to secure. Put onto a baking sheet and brush with the remaining melted butter. Bake in a preheated oven, at 375°F, for 20 minutes, until crisp and lightly browned. Stir 3 tablespoons chopped pistachio nuts into ¼ cup Greek yogurt in a bowl. Serve with the warm pies and a drizzle of honey.

30 Chocolate Cookie and Fruit Squares

Makes 8

4 tablespoons butter, plus extra for greasing

7 oz semisweet chocolate, broken into pieces

1½ tablespoons light corn syrup

⅔ cup coarsely crushed graham crackers or plain cookies

3 tablespoons chopped dried apricots

¼ cup chopped candied cherries

2 tablespoons shredded dried coconut

- Grease a 6 x 6 inch baking pan. Gently heat the butter, 5 oz of the chocolate, and the corn syrup in a saucepan until melted and smooth. Stir in the crushed cookies, apricots, cherries, and coconut until evenly coated in the chocolate. Transfer the mixture to the prepared pan and coarsely spread level.

- Melt the remaining chocolate in a microwave-safe bowl in a microwave on Medium, checking every 30 seconds, until melted and smooth. Drizzle over the cookie mixture. Cover and chill in the freezer for 15 minutes, until firm.

- Cut into 8 squares and serve with coffee.

---

10 Chocolate Dipped Fruits

Melt 3 oz semisweet chocolate, broken into pieces, in a small microwave-safe bowl in a microwave on Medium, checking every 30 seconds, until melted and smooth. Dip a selection of fruit, such as strawberries, cherries, and dried apricots, in the chocolate and place on a baking sheet lined with parchment paper. Chill in the refrigerator for 5 minutes to set.

20 Chocolate Honeycomb Crunch

Melt 2 tablespoons butter in a small saucepan and stir in ½ cup crushed chocolate cookies or chocolate-coated graham crackers. Spoon into the bottom of 2 ramekins and press down firmly with the back of a spoon. Melt together 1 tablespoon honey and 4 oz semisweet chocolate, broken into pieces, in a microwave-safe bowl in a microwave on Medium, checking every 30 seconds, until melted and smooth. Stir in ½ cup mascarpone cheese and spoon over the cookie crusts. Cover and chill in the freezer for 10 minutes. Serve sprinkled with 1 chopped mini chocolate honeycomb toffee (sponge candy) bar.

30 Tropical Fruit and Coconut Cheesecakes

Serves 2

2 tablespoons butter

⅔ cup crushed coconut cookies

½ cup cream cheese

3 tablespoons condensed milk

finely grated rind and juice of
1 lime

2 tablespoons diced pineapple
and mango

- Melt the butter in a small saucepan and stir in the crushed cookies. Divide between 2 dessert glasses and press down with the back of a spoon.

- Mix together the cream cheese, condensed milk, most of the lime rind (reserving a little for decoration), and the lime juice in a bowl. Spoon over the cookie mixture and spread evenly. Cover and chill in the refrigerator for 10 minutes.

- Top with the tropical fruits and reserved lime rind and serve.

 Tropical Fruit Salad with Coconut Cream Put 1 (8 oz) package prepared tropical fruits, ½ piece sliced preserved ginger, and 2 tablespoons preserved ginger syrup from the jar in a bowl and stir well to coat the fruit in the syrup. Mix ¼ cup crème fraîche or Greek yogurt, a pinch of ground ginger, and 1 teaspoon dried coconut in a separate bowl, mix well, and serve with the fruit salad.

 Coconut, Mango, and Lime Layers Divide ⅔ cup crushed coconut cookies between 2 glasses. In a bowl, blend 1 peeled, pitted, and chopped mango with an immersion blender until smooth. Add most of the grated rind (reserving a little for decoration) and all the juice of 1 lime and stir to mix. Beat together ⅓ cup cream cheese and 2 tablespoons condensed milk in a separate bowl until soft, then fold in the mango puree. Spoon half the mango mixture onto the cookies, then repeat the layers. Sprinkle with the reserved lime rind and serve.

 Soft Raspberry Meringues

Serves 4

2 egg whites

½ cup superfine sugar (or the same amount of granulated sugar processed in a food processor for 1 minute)

½ cup raspberries, plus extra to serve

crème fraîche or Greek yogurt, to serve

- Line a large baking sheet with parchment paper. In a clean bowl, whisk the egg whites, using a handheld electric mixer, until stiff. Add the sugar, 1 tablespoon at a time, whisking well between each addition, until firm and glossy.

- Put the raspberries in a bowl and crush with a fork, then lightly fold through the meringue to form a rippled effect. Place large spoonfuls of the mixture on the prepared baking sheet.

- Bake in a preheated oven, at 350°F, for 20 minutes, until firm on the outside. Serve with crème fraîche or Greek yogurt and extra raspberries.

 Mini Baked Alaskas with Raspberries

Put 4 graham crackers or plain cookies on a baking sheet lined with parchment paper and top each with 1 scoop of strawberry ice cream. Place in the freezer. In a clean bowl, whisk 4 egg whites, using a handheld electric mixer, until stiff. Add 1 cup superfine sugar, 1 tablespoon at a time, beating well between each addition, until firm and glossy. Quickly spoon the meringue over the ice cream and cookies, making sure they are completely covered. Place in a preheated oven, at 425°F, for 2–3 minutes, until the meringue is lightly browned. Serve immediately, while the ice cream is still frozen, sprinkled with fresh raspberries.

Floating Islands with Raspberries

In a clean bowl, whisk 2 egg whites, using a handheld electric mixer, until stiff. Add ½ cup superfine sugar, 1 tablespoon at a time, whisking well between each addition, until firm and glossy. Poach spoonfuls of the meringue in a saucepan of simmering water for 2–3 minutes, until firm. Drain with a slotted spoon. Pour a little warmed vanilla pudding over the bottoms of 4 serving bowls, sprinkle with some raspberries, and place the poached meringues on top.

30 Warm Marmalade Cakes

Serves 4

½ cup sunflower spread, plus
  extra for greasing
1 cup all-purpose flour
1 teaspoon baking powder
½ cup firmly packed
  light brown sugar
2 eggs
¼ cup marmalade
2 tablespoons orange juice
¾ cup Grand Marnier
strips of orange rind, to decorate
crème fraîche or whipped cream,
  to serve

- Grease a 7 inch cake pan and line the bottom with parchment paper. Put the flour, baking powder, sugar, sunflower spread, and eggs in a food processor and blend until soft and smooth. Spoon into the prepared pan and bake in a preheated oven, at 350°F, for 20–25 minutes, until lightly browned and firm to the touch.

- Meanwhile, place the marmalade, orange juice, and Grand Marnier in a small saucepan and simmer for a few minutes to make a syrupy sauce.

- Break the cake into pieces, then stack a few pieces in 4 shallow bowls and spoon the marmalade sauce over them.

- Serve with crème fraîche or whipped cream and sprinkled with strips of orange rind to decorate.

---

10 Caramelized Marmalade

Oranges Using a serrated knife, remove the peel and pith from 4 oranges, then cut into thick slices and arrange on 4 serving plates. Heat ¼ cup marmalade, 2 tablespoons orange juice, and 2 tablespoons Grand Marnier in a small saucepan, then simmer for a few minutes until syrupy. Pour the syrup over the oranges and sprinkle with toasted slivered almonds.

20 Sticky Marmalade Microwave Cakes

Beat together ⅔ cup sunflower spread, 1¼ cups all-purpose flour 1 teaspoon baking powder, ¾ cup firmly packed light brown sugar, 2 extra-large eggs, and 2 tablespoons marmalade in a food processor or with a handheld electric mixer until smooth and creamy. Add a little milk if the mixture is too stiff. Place 1 teaspoon marmalade in each of 4 greased microwave-safe individual ramekins. Spoon the sponge batter over the top and cook in a microwave on Medium for 5 minutes. Let stand for 5 minutes, then turn out and serve with cream.

Lemon and Passionfruit Whips

Serves 2

½ cup crushed shortbread cookies
⅔ cup heavy cream
½ cup lemon-flavored yogurt
2 passionfruit, halved

- Divide the crushed cookies between 2 glasses. Whip the cream in a bowl until just thick enough to form soft peaks, then lightly fold in the yogurt with the seeds and pulp from 1 of the passionfruit.

- Spoon the mixture into the glasses and spoon the remaining passionfruit seeds and pulp over the top.

20 Lemon and Passionfruit Syllabubs

Divide the seeds and pulp from 1 halved passionfruit between 2 glasses. Using a handheld electric mixer, whisk together ⅔ cup heavy cream, 3 tablespoons medium-dry white wine, 3 tablespoons superfine sugar, the finely grated rind of ½ lemon, and the seeds and pulp from 1 halved passionfruit in a bowl until the mixture is thick enough to form soft peaks when the whisk is lifted. Spoon into the glasses, cover, and chill for 5–10 minutes. Serve with shortbread cookies.

30 Saucy Lemon and Passionfruit Pudding

Whisk 2 egg yolks, ¼ cup superfine or granulated sugar, and ½ cup milk in a bowl until smooth. Stir in 2 tablespoons all-purpose flour, the grated rind and juice of ½ lemon and, the pulp and seeds of 1 passionfruit. In a clean bowl, whisk 2 egg whites, using a handheld electric mixer, until stiff, then fold into the lemon mixture. Pour into a greased 2½-cup baking dish and place in a roasting pan. Pour boiling water into the pan to come halfway up the side of the dish. Bake in a preheated oven, at 350°F, for 20 minutes, until just lightly browned. Dust with confectioners' sugar and serve immediately, with the sauce that has formed in the bottom of the dish.

MID-DESS-MOB

30 Apple and Blackberry Compote with Almond Scones

Serves 4

3 Granny Smith or other cooking apples, peeled, cored, and sliced
2 tablespoons water
1 cup blackberries
2 tablespoons apricot jam
crème fraîche or other thick cream, to serve

For the scones

1 cup all-purpose flour, plus extra for dusting
1 teaspoon baking powder
½ cup ground almonds (almond meal)
⅓ cup granulated sugar
4 tablespoons butter
⅓ cup milk, plus extra for brushing
1 teaspoon vanilla extract
¼ cup slivered almonds

- To make the scones, put the flour, baking powder, ground almonds, sugar, and butter into a food processor and pulse to make fine crumbs. Add the milk and vanilla extract and pulse to make a soft dough. Turn out the dough onto a floured surface and lightly knead. Press the dough out with your fingers, then stamp out 8 circles using a 3 inch cutter.

- Place the scones on a baking sheet, brush with a little milk, and sprinkle with the slivered almonds. Bake in a preheated oven, at 400°F, for 10–15 minutes, until golden.

- Meanwhile, put the apples into a saucepan with the measured water and cook for 3 minutes, until soft. Stir in the blackberries and apricot preserves and simmer for 1 minute.

- Spoon the compote into 4 shallow bowls, top each with 2 scones and serve with cème fraiche.

 Easy Fruit Compote Cobbler

Warm 1½ cups apple and berry fruit compote in a saucepan for 2 minutes, then transfer to a baking dish. Break 2 bicuits into chunks and sprinkle the fruit over them. Sprinkle with 4 teaspoons demerara or other raw sugar and 2 tablespoons slivered almonds and bake in a preheated oven, at 400°F, for 5 minutes, until hot. Serve with thick cream.

 Fruit Compote with Drop

Biscuits Mix together 1¼ cups all-purpose flour, 1 teaspoon baking powder, a large pinch of salt, and 4 teaspoons granulated sugar in a bowl. Make a well in the center, then add 1 extra-large egg. Gradually add ⅔ cup milk, whisking continuously to make a smooth, thick batter. Heat a little butter in a large skillet, add spoonfuls of the batter, and cook until set and lightly browned underneath.

Turn the biscuits over and cook for another 30 seconds. Repeat with the remaining batter to make about 8 biscuits. Meanwhile, put 3 peeled, cored and chopped Granny Smith or other cooking apples in a saucepan with ¼ cup granulated sugar and ¼ cup water. Simmer for 3 minutes, until soft, then stir in 1 cup blackberries and cook for 1 minute. Sprinkle the biscuits with slivered almonds and serve warm with the fruit compote.

Pan-Fried Peach and Plum Cinnamon Crunch

Serves 4

6 tablespoons butter

4 peaches, halved, pitted and cut into wedges

6 plums, halved and pitted

¼ cup firmly packed light brown sugar

1 teaspoon ground cinnamon

4 graham crackers or other plain cookies, crushed

ice cream, to serve

- Heat half the butter in a large, flameproof skillet, add the peaches, plums, and sugar, and simmer gently for 5 minutes, turning occasionally, until soft.

- In a separate saucepan, melt the remaining butter and stir in the cinnamon. Add the crushed crackers or cookies and stir to coat. Sprinkle the mixture over the peaches and plums.

- Place the skillet under a preheated medium broiler and cook for 5 minutes, until lightly browned and crunchy. Serve with ice cream.

Peach and Plum Waffles

Heat 4 tablespoons butter in a skillet, add 2 halved, pitted, and sliced peaches, 6 halved, pitted, and chopped plums, ¼ cup granulated sugar, and 1 teaspoon ground cinnamon, and cook for 5 minutes, until the fruit is soft and the juices syrupy. Warm 8 waffles in the toaster or under a preheated broiler, then serve with the warm fruit and spoonfuls of Greek yogurt or whipped cream.

Peach and Plum Clafoutis

Place 2 halved, pitted, and sliced peaches and 4 halved, pitted, and chopped plums in a greased shallow 1¼ quart baking dish. Put 4 eggs, ½ cup granulated sugar, ⅔ cup all-purpose flour, 1 teaspoon ground cinnamon, 2½ cups milk, and 4 tablespoons melted butter in a food processor or blender and blend to make a smooth batter. Pour the batter over the fruit and bake in a preheated oven, at 375°F, for 25 minutes, until lightly browned and set. Serve dusted with confectioners' sugar.

30 Apple and Peach Marzipan Slice

Serves 2

½ sheet of ready-to-bake puff pastry

1 sweet, crisp apple, such as Pippin or Golden Delicious, peeled, cored, and coarsely grated

1 peach, halved, pitted, and chopped

1 oz coarsely grated marzipan

beaten egg, to glaze

2 teaspoons granulated sugar

confectioners' sugar, for dusting

custard or cream, to serve

- Put the pastry on a baking sheet and add the apple along one side. Top with the peach and sprinkle with the marzipan.

- Brush the edge of the pastry with a little beaten egg, fold the pastry over the filling, and press the edges with the back of a fork to seal. Cut a few slashes across the top of the pastry, brush with beaten egg, and sprinkle with the granulated sugar.

- Bake in a preheated oven, at 400°F, for 20 minutes, until crisp and lightly browned. Dust with confectioners' sugar, then slice and serve with custard or cream.

 Broiled Marzipan Peaches

Place 2 halved and pitted peaches, cut side up, in a small, shallow flameproof dish. Mix together 1 oz chopped marzipan and 2 crushed plain cookies in a bowl, then spoon the mixture over the peaches. Drizzle with honey and cook under a preheated medium broiler for 5 minutes, until soft and the marzipan is melted and bubbling. Sprinkle with a few chopped pecans and serve with cream.

 Apple and Peach Marzipan Crisp

Place 1 peeled, cored, and chopped apple with 1 tablespoon water in a saucepan and cook for 3 minutes, until soft. Stir in 1 halved, pitted, and chopped peach and 2 tablespoons apricot preserves. Transfer the mixture to a small ovenproof dish. Meanwhile, melt 2 tablespoons butter in a separate saucepan, add 1 tablespoon light corn syrup, ½ cup rolled oats, 1 oz chopped marzipan, and 1 tablespoon chopped pecans, and mix well. Sprinkle the mixture over the fruit and bake in a preheated oven, at 375°F, for 10 minutes, until crisp. Serve with cream or ice cream.

30 Orange and Pistachio Cornmeal Muffins with Dates

Serves 2

⅓ cup all-purpose flour

⅓ cup cornmeal

¼ cup granulated sugar, plus 2 tablespoons

½ teaspoon baking powder

1 egg, beaten

2 tablespoons butter, melted

grated rind and juice of 1 orange

2 tablespoons coarsely chopped shelled pistachio nuts

1 fresh date, pitted and coarsely chopped

- Line 4 cups of a muffin pan with paper muffin liners. Sift the flour into a bowl, then add the cornmeal, the ¼ cup granulated sugar, and the baking powder. In a small bowl, mix together the egg, melted butter, and orange rind, then pour the wet ingredients into the dry ingredients and stir until just combined. Add 1 tablespoon of the pistachios.

- Spoon the batter into the prepared muffin pan and bake in a preheated oven, at 350°F, for 15–20 minutes, until lightly browned, risen, and cooked through.

- Meanwhile, put the orange juice and remaining sugar into a saucepan and bring to a boil, then reduce the heat and simmer for 2 minutes, until syrupy.

- Remove the muffins from the oven and pierce each 3–4 times with a toothpick, then pour 1 tablespoon of the syrup over each. Serve sprinkled with the coarsely chopped date and remaining pistachios.

 Simple Date and Pistachio Oranges Using a serrated knife, remove the peel and pith from 3 oranges, then cut into slices. Put into a bowl with 6 pitted and coarsely chopped fresh dates, 2 tablespoons honey, and 2 tablespoons coarsely chopped pistachio nuts. Serve with ice cream or crème fraîche.

 Orange Cornmeal Pancakes with Dates and Pistachios Put ½ cup cornmeal, 1 tablespoon all-purpose flour, and ½ teaspoon baking powder in a bowl. Add 1 beaten egg and the finely grated rind and juice of 1 orange and mix well. Heat a little butter in a skillet, add large tablespoons of the batter, well spaced apart, and cook for 1 minute, then flip over using a spatula and cook for about 1 minute until lightly browned. Repeat with the remaining batter to make 6 pancakes. Serve drizzled with honey and sprinkled with 2 tablespoons pitted and coarsely chopped fresh dates and 2 tablespoons coarsely chopped pistachio nuts.

Pan-Fried Banana and Maple Syrup Brioche Rolls

Serves 2

2 eggs, beaten
½ cup milk
1 teaspoon vanilla extract
½ teaspoon ground cinnamon
4 thin slices of brioche
1 ripe banana
1 tablespoon maple syrup, plus
   extra to drizzle
2 tablespoons butter
vanilla yogurt, to serve

- Beat together the eggs, milk, vanilla extract, and cinnamon in a shallow dish until well blended. Place the brioche slices in the egg mixture and let soak for 2 minutes.

- Mash together the banana and maple syrup in a separate bowl. Carefully remove the slices of brioche from the egg mixture and place on a board. Divide the banana mixture among the slices and spread to within the edges. Roll up and secure each with a toothpick.

- Heat the butter in a skillet. Using a spatula, carefully place each roll in the skillet and cook for 4–5 minutes, until lightly browned, turning halfway through cooking. Serve hot with spoonfuls of vanilla yogurt and drizzled with maple syrup.

 Brioche Toasts with Banana and Maple Syrup Beat together 1 egg, ⅓ cup milk and ½ teaspoon vanilla extract in a shallow dish. Dip 2 slices of brioche into the mixture. Heat 2 tablespoons butter in a skillet, add the brioche slices, and cook for 2 minutes on each side, until lightly browned. Slice 1 banana and arrange on top of each, then drizzle with maple syrup. Serve with spoonfuls of vanilla yogurt.

 Brioche, Banana, and Maple Syrup Pudding Lightly butter 4 slices of brioche, then cut in half diagonally. Toss 1 thinly sliced banana with 2 tablespoons maple syrup in a bowl. In a small, shallow ovenproof dish, layer the brioche slices with the bananas. Beat together 2 eggs, ⅔ cup milk, and 1 teaspoon vanilla extract in a small bowl. Slowly pour the milk mixture over the brioche, letting the bread soak it up. Bake in the top of a preheated oven, at 400°F, for 20 minutes, until lightly browned and just firm. Serve hot with vanilla yogurt.

Pan-Fried Marsala Fruit and Almonds

Serves 2

2 tablespoons unsalted butter

1 peach, halved, pitted, and quartered

1 nectarine, halved, pitted ,and quartered

4 apricots, halved and pitted

2 tablespoons packed light brown sugar

2 tablespoons marsala

1 tablespoon honey

3 tablespoons toasted slivered almonds

vanilla ice cream, to serve

- Heat the butter in a skillet, add the fruit, and cook over medium-high heat for 3–4 minutes, until softened and lightly browned in places, turning once or twice.

- Add the sugar and cook, gently tossing, for another 1 minute, then add the marsala. Heat, stirring, for 1 minute, then add the honey and almonds and stir to coat. Serve with scoops of vanilla ice cream.

10 Pan-Fried Apricots with Almonds

Heat 2 tablespoons butter in a skillet, add 8 halved and pitted apricots, and cook over medium heat, cut side down, for 2–3 minutes. Sprinkle with 3 tablespoons packed light brown sugar and 1 tablespoon honey and cook over low heat for another 2–3 minutes, turning occasionally. Sprinkle with 1 tablespoon toasted slivered almonds and serve hot with ice cream or crème fraîche.

30 Baked Almond Peaches and

Nectarines Halve and pit 2 peaches and 2 nectarines and place in a shallow, ovenproof dish. Put 2 tablespoons butter and 2 tablespoons packed light brown sugar in a saucepan and gently stir and heat until smooth and syrupy. Add 1 tablespoon marsala and stir again until smooth, then drizzle the sauce over the peaches. Grate 2 oz marzipan and sprinkle it over the fruit, then sprinkle with ¼ cup slivered almonds. Bake in a preheated oven, at 350°F, for 20 minutes, until soft and lightly browned in places. Serve with crème fraîche, if desired.

 Baked Chocolate Orange Mousse

Serves 4

8 oz milk chocolate,
  broken into pieces
1 stick butter
2 eggs
3 tablespoons superfine
  or granulated sugar
finely grated rind of 1 orange, plus
  extra pared rind to decorate
confectioners' sugar, for dusting

- Melt the chocolate and butter in a heatproof bowl set over a saucepan of gently simmering water, making sure the bottom of the bowl does not touch the water. Let cool slightly.

- Combine the eggs and superfine or granulated sugar in a bowl and beat together, using a handheld electric mixer, until thick. Carefully fold in the orange rind, then the melted chocolate mixture.

- Spoon the mixture into 4 large ramekins and bake in a preheated oven, at 350°F, for 15 minutes, until the tops are just set.

- Let cool for 2 minutes, then sprinkle with the pared orange rind. Serve warm dusted with a little confectioners' sugar.

 Speedy Chocolate Orange Creams

Melt together 8 oz milk chocolate, broken into pieces, and ¾ cup heavy cream in a heatproof bowl set over a saucepan of gently simmering water, stirring until smooth and melted. Let cool slightly. Lightly crush a 4 oz orange chocolate candy bar and divide among 4 glasses. Pour the chocolate cream over the top and chill for 5 minutes before serving.

 Chilled Chocolate and Orange Mousse

Melt 5 oz milk chocolate, broken into pieces, in a heatproof bowl set over a saucepan of gently simmering water, then let cool slightly. Add 4 egg yolks and stir well. In a clean bowl, whisk 4 egg whites with a handheld electric mixer until stiff, then gently fold into the chocolate mixture with the finely grated rind of 1 orange. Divide among 4 glasses and chill for at least 5 minutes before serving.

Index

Acknowledgments

Recipes by: **Emma Jane Frost and Nichola Palmer**
Executive Editor: **Eleanor Maxfield**
Managing Editor: **Clare Churly**
Art Direction: **Tracy Killick and Geoff Fennell for Tracy Killick Art Direction and Design**
Original Design Concept: **www.gradedesign.com**
Designer: **Tracy Killick Art Direction and Design**
Photographer: **Lis Parsons**
Home Economist: **Emma Jane Frost**
Prop Stylist: **Liz Hippisley**
Senior Production Manager: **Katherine Hockley**